CHAOS
IN
AMERICA

★ ★ ★

John L. King

Library of Congress Cataloging-in-Publication Data

King, John L. (John Lafayette), 1917-1990
    Chaos in America / by John L. King
        p.   cm.
    ISBN 0-922356-24-6: $11.95
    1. Debts, Public—United States—History.
    2. Money—United States—History.
    I. Title.
HJ8032.A2K56 1990
336.3'4'0973—dc20

                                                        90-14449
                                                        CIP

Published by
AMERICA WEST PUBLISHERS
P.O. Box 3300
Bozeman, MT 59772

Cover design by: Randy Singleton

Printed in the United States of America
10 9 8 7 6 5 4 3

"Things fall apart, the center cannot hold."

— Yeats

"If the present growth trends in world population, industrialization, pollution, food production, and resource depletion continue unchanged, the limits to growth on this planet will be reached sometime within the next hundred years. The most probable result will be a rather sudden and uncontrollable decline in both population and industrial capacity."

— The Limits to Growth
Rome, 1972

"The harvest is past
the summer is ended
And we are not saved."

— Jeremiah

TABLE OF CONTENTS

PREFACE

Has America gone from riches to rags? Has America become a nation in an irreversible economic decline? Could America face national bankruptcy? Is the industrial era now ending? If any or all of these events are in our future, then any one, or all, could bring along vast social, cultural, and political changes. This book is about the possibility that epic change is now in the making which encompasses any, or all, of these scenarios.

The public credit, the debts of Uncle Sam, have a curious detached irrelevance for all of us. We have a "So what?" attitude about them. This is probably because investors in government securities have been conditioned by long experience to believe that bad news is heaven-sent. The worse things have gotten for the government's debts, the more the bondholders seem to have liked it. For example, when the economy fell into recession, interest rates fell all the while the federal deficit continued to rise. A bizarre behavior.

However, when the economic credit system contracts, as it is now, old rules and belief systems are forced to change. Now we will be compelled to take a cold, hard look at the tens of billions of dollars of contingent liabilities of Uncle Sam that one day might become due and payable. What then? The government would have to issue more securities, of course. But would Wall Street, or foreigners, buy them? Would the Federal Reserve try to monetize them? What is going to happen to all of us? This is what this book is about.

I outline in detail how federal debts could put America on a path to national bankruptcy like other nations have before us. The book stresses the uncontrollable and disastrous rise in interest rates which this chart depicts. Interest makes these debts terribly unmanageable. Why couldn't we have been smarter? Done something sooner about steadily growing interest so we would not be in this fix?

Because our techniques for dealing with federal deficits, as they grew, was a process that produced interest on current interest at a compound rate higher than the other components of the Gross National Product, thereby siphoning off growth. The problem grew as politicians were unable or unwilling to raise taxes. If they had done this, the heavier taxes on the public would have caused them to default sooner on the $9 trillion in debts they owed.

Thus, if we had taxed ourselves to pay the debtors, we would have all gone back a little. But if we repudiate the debt, as we must, that is the end of our credit system.

The creditworthiness of the Federal Government is the foundation of the credit system in America. For example, U.S. Treasury Bonds serve as collateral for Federal Reserve Notes (cash), one debt supporting another. Thus, if the Bonds became worthless, so would the paper money, and so would the private credit system's paper obligations—representations of wealth, but not wealth. It would be a form of financial doomsday.

The book explains the problem, and predicts, based on history, some potential outcomes and how Americans might live in the early part of the twenty-first century. This epic change could transform America and the way we live in it tomorrow.

The book traces the decline of America which actually started after World War II's economic boom faltered in the 1960s. America grew for awhile, then started down the economic slope. This idea of America in decline has been written about, but always with a happy ending, that America will not end as Rome did, but will, after a prolonged time, perhaps be like England is today. None of the "decline" authors predicted the chance of a national debt default nor the epic change it would bring.

America's power, like that of other empires preceding it, began to wane around the early 1960s. Gradually, as time went on, American industry lost its global share of markets; there was a global shift to service industries, and the financial services industry in America exploded. The result of this convergence of events was a root change in the American experience. The lives of the public were being radically altered, and this effect on their psyche began to be seen in changes in social events—Rambo movies, and other bullish-good news type entertainment, peaked and slid into oblivion; the moral decline continued, and accelerated. Historically, similar signs that other falling empires also experienced on their way to oblivion were seen in America. The public, as in Rome, believed any change would be corrected and things would return to the old norms.

Crucially, the American financial/ethical system was rooted in the *promises men live by*. These promises are interwoven and are expressed and implied, too. For example, a worker advances his work for a week in the expectation that the employer will carry out his promise to pay the agreed upon wage. And this promise-system was all pervasive. For it to succeed, as it did for all of American history, it was essential that the promises be fulfilled. Perhaps the sanctity of this promise-contract may well have been the greatest single influence in our economic system for our continued progress. When this chain of promises is broken with national bankruptcy, then the economic system will be in a massive convulsion. The system that delivered the wealth will be terminal.

The convergence of a financial panic, a moral breakdown, a government perhaps plunging into bankruptcy, and cultural dislocations are flashing yellow lights of an unparalleled transformation going on in America.

Since the sharp rise in oil prices in the mid-seventies which distorted world economic events and, in turn, focused the public's attention on economic and financial matters, our lives have been slowly changing. Because of that event and many additional factors, the American public began to direct much of their attention to the acquisition of money—searching for higher yields, a better deal, financial security, etc. Confidence in the American system was subtly being replaced by greed.

Before this change, however, we had seen the generational changes of the late 1960s—the peace movement, opposition to the Vietnam war—a new generation that was looking for and demanding change. Many thought this was an aberration, but instead the seeds planted back then are now growing wherever we look. Now the public is demonstrating for or against everything under the sun, from abortion to dirty water to scandals in high office.

From this ferment we now see all around us systemic problems of inequality, sexism, corporate power, militarism, health care systems, overfilled prisons, and so on. Obviously this was not the America of the textbook American tradition. It was something new and scary.

For many years my own background has been in economic history and especially the history of money. More accurately, the history of credit and debt, since this is preponderantly our "money system" (though most people still believe it is paper money and coins).

At any rate, in the credit/debt sector some very bad events were taking place. They did not start yesterday. The train of events that is leading us into what might be a devastating economic tomorrow started with government monetary and fiscal policies of the 1930s. For years we all believed that those affairs rested on rock solid ground. Now we are learning that those very same processes have reached the point where they could destroy America as we knew it. It could be difficult to stop this tidal wave.

We are entering a time of more rapid change. Eric Hoffer wrote, "We can never be prepared for that which is wholly new. We have to adjust ourselves, and very radical adjustment is a crisis in self-esteem—we undergo a test, we have to prove ourselves. It needs inordinate self-confidence to face drastic change without inner trembling. [That] we can never be fit and ready for that which is wholly new has some peculiar results. A population undergoing drastic change is a population of misfits...unbalanced, explosive, and hungry for action is how they prove their worth and it will plunge into an orgy of action."[1]

So, the time has come to take a penetrating look at our recent American past so we can prepare ourselves for a very new future for us all.

We are starting sweeping changes in the way we will live in the near future, which could also change the consciousness of the average American. For example, up until now the average person has never been more loyal to the doctrine of individualism and unhampered private enterprise. But that is ending and there will emerge a clash between capital and labor. Until now, this has remained inaudible—but this is only because the nation's economic mechanism has seemed to most of us to run with the oil of prosperity. Now that is gone. Change is underway.

It is my feeling that the American-cult-belief of keeping a stiff upper lip, of singing in the rain, where the public hates to admit that things are not going well, will be demolished in the trying times we are now in.

Where can we see signs of the American economy in savage decline? Signs of change abound: in economic activity and the current social, cultural, and political changes of unparalleled scale. Briefly:

ECONOMIC ACTIVITY

We are either in a long and total Depression now or very near it. However, unlike the 1930s, the American economic system has changed fundamentally during the last generation from a financially liquid society, where it was easy to borrow and lend and we had hoards of gold, to an illiquid society, one buried in debt and removed from gold and financial sanity, thrift, and prudence in our business affairs.

The Depression could be precipitated and intensified by leverage (paying little down on large loans) in credit creation, thus incurring a gigantic debt load which we are unable to repay at every level: consumers, corporations, cities, and states, and perhaps even federal debts. The debts are being settled in devastating hard times...going unpaid in large measure.

The American economic/financial system ran like a runaway rocket in the days leading to a Money Panic, this Panic will bring us soaring interest rates, falling stock and bond prices, and real estate prices near total collapse. A sort of financial doomsday may be ahead.

It could be that the Industrial Revolution and the economic and financial systems it developed may all be vanishing to be replaced by some system that will be different, very different. The old "bigger is better" idea could be replaced by "small is better."

SOCIAL

The aging of the American population seems to promise trouble with the Social Security system. It was planned and funded in an era when people died younger. Now, the old are a burden. An old economic truism is that when six people work to support four, all is well, but when four people work to support six, the system is ready for anarchy. That is where we could be heading. This is just another sign of social breakdown. There are others:

Crime, drugs, sexual freedom—all signs of a social and moral breakdown, much like other civilizations before America.

Our past "greed society" developed in Americans a feeling of mistrust, envy, ego, and animosity where it became increasingly difficult to conduct any kind of business or other affair. Haven't you noticed how hard it is just to get along with people?

CULTURAL

The growing disrespect, starting about 1968, for authority among all levels of the population surfaced. A new set of emerging values that abandoned respect for law and order signaled root change in our affairs. But we were told this was an aberration, not "real." We were told that it would soon be over.

This move into a new form of society has its parallel in past history with the gigantic change from the Middle Ages way of life to that of life in the Industrial Age, which we may be leaving.

POLITICAL

There is also a growing breakdown in the political forces that manage the public institutions and dictate our rules of law. Increasingly, they made rash and inept decisions on affairs that impacted us all—insignificant grape scares and watermelon scares in our food distribution chain and toxic chemical spills, oil tanker spills, etc. were only an early sign of other growing political ineptness. The authorities in Washington and in our cities and states became increasingly unable to manage public affairs: the regulations they created failed, they deregulated our money industries, and created a devilish monster which put our money in grave jeopardy. Lastly, it was common for political figures to be indicted for fraud and nefarious ways, but no one gave it much thought...casual crime in high places, very much the same as in the Roman Empire when it started its sixth century downfall.

Our downfall, by contrast, will happen within our own life-times, so we can see it all going on and have a chance to prepare our own lives for tomorrow. This is what this book is all about.

In subsequent chapters, I deal at length with each of these major topics describing how each area has changed over the years, and what the meaning of this could be for all of us in the days to come.

We all want to know the future. Through history we have learned that in a general way it is possible to forecast general long-range trends such as the impact of the Industrial Revolution; the process of urbanization; or the life cycle of a revolution. But this is a mile away from our current electronic lifestyles and predictions.

I speculate that daily life *tomorrow* will be no bed of roses. But it will be excitingly different, and Americans will cope with the new change as they have done with past changes. Americans have a flair for can-do and sacrifice and adapting and coping with all sorts of changes. Tomorrow is a time of promise, not despair.

But one of the threads running through this books is that, like other civilizations before us, America and the world could be seeing the end of the Industrial Revolution and the lifestyles it brought. Signs are emerging that we are near an epochal turning point—lunging into something very new and different from anything we, and the world, have known before.

TRANSCENDENTAL CHANGE

The change described in this book might be deeper and more pervasive than any change in America since the beginning. It may be the most fateful for the world, especially in the long history of industrial society. And the convulsion is near. In 1989, major changes erupted in Germany and other countries on the Russian periphery, and in Russia itself. Americans were curiously detached from this change, feeling that they were isolated from it.

In America, our industrial society is rooted in the long-term modernization trend that emerged some ten centuries ago. We organized around impersonal, utilitarian values rather than being shaped by traditional cultural and religious values. The past era marked the beginning of the idea of material progress accompanied by the technological revolution in modern science.

But there is now growing resistance to all aspects of this

long-term trend. The industrial society led to ever-increasing use of resources and a technology that was big and exploitive, person-intimidating and person-replacing. Now we are entering an age of countertrend: small technology, resource-saving, environmentally benign, and under control of those of us that use it. We are starting to reverse the old trend of our recent past in which a growing number of people became superfluous as producers.

We are in a major departure from that old industrial society to a new society. And it will be hard times that will provide the catalyst for this change.

When moral decay sets in a society, the society will not long endure. We have had ample evidence of this in America with growing drug use, sex abuse and cheating and stealing in high places, etc. De Toqueville believed that America became great because America was good, and that when America ceased to be good, America would cease to be great.

But this view is a far cry from mainstream views in America in 1990. Instead of decay and collapse, ideas which were derided as "Spenglerian gloom and views of latter-day Jeremiahs," it was suggested by the author "that for the foreseeable future, powerful industrial economic and demographic forces will be converging in a way that will offer a welcome respite from the traumas of the past two decades."[2] Not only that, "but a third industrial revolution" is in the making.

The realities of history are unrelenting. Rather than more growth and more good news, there could probably be less growth and more bad news. That is, as the cliche goes, "as sure as death and taxes." This may be because societies have always had to finally deal with debt and that has entailed hard times and dramatic change. This change could be more pervasive and more widespread in America than anything most people can now imagine.

There is nothing in history to suggest that a social transformation such as that suggested in this book could happen without the most severe economic and social disruptions and systems breakdowns. It will not be easy getting from here to there as Americans will discover in the decade of the 1990s.

But in the wake of this change there will be exciting new ways of doing old things—new lifestyles, new challenges, new hope and a new way of resolving old problems. This will be an era of hope and challenge for us all.

PREFACE

REFERENCES

1. Hoffer, Eric, *The Ordeal of Change* (Harper & Row, N.Y.C., 1963), p. 31.

2. Morris, Charles R., "The Coming Global Boom," *Atlantic,* October 1989, pp. 56-91.

FORWARD

Lenin wrote, "Germany will arm herself out of existence, the British Empire will expand herself out of existence, and the United States will loan herself out of existence." Lenin may have been right. America now owes, perhaps, over $20 trillion in debt—$11 trillion is federal government on-and-off budget debts; consumers, corporations and cities and states owe, collectively, $9 trillion. The problem, simply, is where are we going to get the funds to pay back all of this borrowed money? This is important because all through history, debts are always paid, either by the debtor or the creditor. But they are paid.

In America we seem to be unable to avoid a future financial precipice since we have been on a debt road that leads nowhere else since the end of World War II. What will happen to all of us now?

We are now in the worst recession since 1980-1982. And there is an even chance this recession could spill over into a depression. Why? Because the powerful deflationary forces of falling wages and prices, now so widespread, started years ago, but since their collective impact was silent and slow, this deflation went unnoticed. It now has the capability of changing the character of this recession into something far worse. A big reason for this is that we were addicted as a nation to greed and money, so nothing else mattered except the next "deal."

As a society we have ignored Biblical warnings as well. St. Paul wrote, "god chose what is foolish in the world to shame the

wise, God chose what is weak in the world to shame the strong."
(1 Cor. 1:27). So, going into debt was easy, and we did. But
falling prices are now everywhere—everything we need is now
cheaper, and it is as old as time that when prices fall the rich
grow poor. That is because if you assume debts when prices are
high, you are bound to have difficulty paying off those same
debts when prices fall and cash flows also fall.

We lived on credit in America. We borrowed and we spent,
and we pledged our future earning power into eternity since we
all believed things would always get better. Not only better, but a
lot better. As a nation we believed that the repayment of our
debts would be easy with rising incomes and good times always
just ahead. After all, that was "the American way." Why did we
do this? Because, as Walter Lippman, an astute observer of
America wrote a long time ago, "Men respond as forceful to
fictions as to realities, even those they themselves created."
What we imagined determined what we did—so we imagined
perpetual prosperity and we acted on that error. But since facts
are always born free and equal, we must now face the facts.

The reality may be now are that the days of American growth
and material well-being may be behind us. One of the main
themes of this book is that they might not return for awhile since
the period we might enter will be no replay of Great Depression
I. It may be something terrifyingly new and very different.

What has gone wrong?

Credit historically has always passed from strong hands to
weak hands. Thus, our government for many years, for example,
has extended vast credits to the farm community (and others)
who over our history have repeatedly had difficulty paying back
their obligations. Corporations loaned vast sums to consumers
who traditionally found themselves unable to repay the loans
they assumed. From one sector to another, the end result was
always the same: bankruptcy.

Yet, in America's past, credit has, over time, performed a
wonderful function: it has raised the standard of living in America

to historical heights—never have so many people had such a plethora of material goods. But, this is also a historical curiosity since the standard of living for most people on the globe has been low for centuries. Will we now rediscover this reality in America? We might. It is too early to have any definite signals now.

What is so terribly wrong with debts? It is the powerful role played by compound interest. Compound interest makes debts, in most cases, impossible to repay because the progression of compound interest is not arithmetic, 1,2,3,4, as most people think it is, but geometric, 2,4,8,16. And interest is relentless and unforgiving. A simple idea to help understand the power of interest is that of the Rule of 72. This means you divide a rate of interest into the number 72 and it will tell you how long before the sums double: thus, 8% goes into 72 9 times, so in 9 years $1,000 becomes $2,000. This may seem trivial, but it is not at all when people buy houses involving large credit sums extended at high rates of interest. It does not take long before their inability to repay the debts and high interest becomes apparent to the homeowner. Now we are in the middle of an extraordinary real estate liquidation because too many buyers of homes were ignorant of the simple Rule of 72 and the power of compound interest.

In the corporate sector in America, in the 1980s, mergers involving billions of dollars became the new financial activity as it had many times before in our historical past. Compound interest crippled virtually every one of the leveraged buy-out deals. The reality is that compound interest did the mergers in because in an economic slowdown interest payments must be made while dividends can be postponed. Inability to pay interest has already sunk many of our leading corporations. And others, buried in debt, are sure to follow, which always leads to sharply rising unemployment.

We might soon see the Latin loans go unpaid for the exact same reasons. In Latin America, four great economic expansions ended in the financial crises of 1825, 1873, 1890 and 1929. These huge financial crisis cycles all had the same cause: the structure of banks lending for profit. In the conventional telling, however, the wayward action of the borrowing nations was traditionally blamed. The Latin boom was tied to the expanding phase of the international business cycle, and the huge American and foreign bank loans triggered a temporary prosperity in Latin America. But a slowdown now in American economic activity will lead soon, if it has not already, to a financial debacle with the Latin loans. In the past when this has happened civil strife erupted in Latin America and most governments down there saw it as the better part of wisdom to concede power to the military.

It is not a radical assumption to believe that in a reasonable time the Latin debts will finally go into default. When this happens a global monetary crisis will be unavoidable—the loans that will not be paid back will inflict permanent damage on the world banking system. That may be ahead. You may not want to think this will happen, but it has happened four times since 1825 and now is the fifth time. When it does, you had better be prepared and an important message of this book is just how you can prepare your own personal finances for major financial problems ahead.

All through U.S. history our banks and Latin leaders have failed to anticipate the downswing in economic activity that invariably follows the upswing which demonstrates a certain historical amnesia. But the reality of our economic system is that few will sit on the sidelines during an expansion. Growth breeds over-optimism and the self-reinforcing delusion of permanence which is always followed by a rude awakening and a panic.

We will learn again in this country that no economy in all of economic history has ever been so productive that it can generate enough wealth to pay off a huge percentage of its capacity in interest charges. Yet, the public has always believed that this could be done.

RATIO OF DEBT TO NATIONAL INCOME

One mainstream argument that large federal debts are manageable was to cite the ratio of any given budget deficit year to the national income of that year. Thus, it was said in 1989 that ratio of debt to national income was just 2.6%, one-half of what the ratio was in 1982.[1] That was perceived to be "good news" by the authors of *Megatrends 2000.*

But this analysis is seriously flawed and false since national income (profits, wages, farm income, etc.) is precisely the item that falls like a rock when hard times emerge, as we are seeing now. In great Depression I, national income fell by 60%, but debts by only 14%, so the debt loads actually became heavier back then as they are right now for so many Americans.

RATIO OF DEBT TO GNP

Another comparison is that of debt to Gross National Product since GNP is the only real measure of where all wealth to repay debts originates. At the bottom of the last Great Depression the ratio was 260%, and by 1989, just before our present crisis, it had risen to 240%, signalling we were reaching a debt plateau that could not be sustained. But borrowing continued unchecked.

As our form of economic society—capitalism—matured, there was a subtle shift in economic activity from making goods to making money. And since our money is debt-money, we now can see the result of this shift in aggregation debts being seven to ten times larger than equity in America. So, as our financial sector capsizes, so could our economy.

RATIO OF GOVERNMENT RECEIPTS TO NET INTEREST EXPENSE

Still another comparison is that of the Federal Governments' receipts to its net interest expense. In 1987 the ratio was 6.2%,

xvi ■ John L. King

the lowest ratio of receipts to interest expense since 1947 falling from 11.9% in 1977. Was this an important new trend? No. And in this book I explain why this is irrelevant.

These various comparisons reveal nothing because in a depressed time like the present all revenues and income sources decline and the one thing that does not fall down is the level of debt and interest payments on that debt. We can see that now: debts are higher and incomes and cash flows are low, so, in real terms, the debt loads are far more burdensome, unwieldy and impossible to repay.

ROOTING THROUGH THE ASHES IN THE DARK

In early 1990, the Bush Administration announced its budget for fiscal year 1991, which started October 1, 1990, of $1.23 trillion. A number that should have stifled any notion that talk was cheap. This chart depicts the outlays—and net interest payments are the third largest item. As our present recession deepens, payments to individuals and military spending will decline, but net interest payments can only grow, becoming the number one problem instead of number three.

Beyond that, the politicians also forecast in that budget that interest rates would drop substantially, short-term rates would fall from an average of 8% in 1989 to 4.4% by 1994. But, at the time this prediction was made, in early 1990, interest rates had already risen globally and in America. What this budget forecast time has proven to be disastrously wrong.

Interest costs had a large importance to the federal government budget planners because the on-budget debts were nearly $3 trillion (not to mention off-budget debts of almost another $2.5 trillion, according to the General Accounting Office), and in 1990 interest payments were estimated to be about $175 billion— and growing. They were actually closer to $50 billion higher since revenues from the Social Security Trust Fund were being used to disguise the true size of the deficits. As a rough rule-of-thumb, whenever interest rates average 1% higher than predicted, the federal budget gap will widen by at least $11 billion within a year, and by even greater amounts in subsequent years. [2] This means trouble is being brewed for the future.

But, during all of the talks about the size of the budget, little notice was given by the politicians, media, or economic experts to the role of compound interest on soaring debt levels. So, again, we are forced to return to debt which always commences a destructive cycle of compound interest payments which demand still more debt for their service. Because of this, you will read we could evolve into a new economic system where the debts are settled in ways that do not involve the payment of interest similar to that of the Moslem religion. We could in time come to regard the payment of interest as blasphemy.

We know by now also that our federal government can do nothing to halt the liquidation of debts. But we believed, like a religion, in our government as being super-powerful, capable of accomplishing anything for us, including help with our debts being liquidated. Alas, it was not able to do this. We forgot, too, that it was also run by other human beings who also fail just like the rest of us.

But, now is a very different time and more dangerous for us than the debt liquidations of the last Great Depression because of a root change in our government's finances. In the 1930s Uncle Sam was creditworthy, had vast hoards of gold, and could easily borrow to finance government rescue agencies.

Now, however, Uncle Sam's own finances are in the worst disarray in U.S. history. We have all also forgotten that America started out with a worthless currency—the ill-fated Continental paper money issued to finance the Revolutionary War. Now we see major changes in our society which, if they occur, could cause another worthless currency to emerge. This is because the U.S. paper dollar (Federal Reserve Note) is supported by the credit of Uncle Sam which might get into trouble, God forbid! And, if the government's credit is finally determined in the marketplace to be no good, then our paper money (which has Treasury Bonds as collateral) will also become throwaway paper. What do we do then? I have some suggestions dealing with this untoward happening.

The ongoing deflation, and debt liquidation will continue unabated, and could change radically our way of life. No one wants to think that, of course. We want a happy ending like in a fairy story. But we have lived on borrowed time and borrowed money, and now the Piper is there for payment. We cannot pay back what we all owe on our debts. We have exhausted our creditworthiness at every level. We will, therefore, pay our debts back in defaults, foreclosures, liquidations such as we see on the rise all over America now. This is how debts have been settled from the beginning of economic time. For Americans, it was easier back in the 1930s, bad as that was, compared to now because we are virtually out of resources, our wealth has been pledged into eternity and we are unable to repay all we owe.

Because the U.S. dollar was the symbol of strength and the world reserve currency since the Bretton Woods agreement, most industrialized nations main bank reserve holdings are now in U.S. dollars. The dollars could fall sharply in value. So, the recession times will be spread abroad.

If the economic system breaks down, it may not be smooth. It could be filled with bumps and turns because our electronic monies are at great risk, being totally dependent on our vast electronic communication systems which themselves are over-taxed before this crisis.[3] Any computer outage could cause the electronic credit monies to vanish and worsen the solution of many credit problems.

There is no one cause of our present travail. An economic slowdown, like the present, is caused by a convergence of events that now seems almost planned by some greater Power and some refer to the Biblical Revelations for reference. A bank credit collapse was at the heart of Great Depression I—but that was then; and this is now.

One thing that does not cause depressions is the maldistribution of income. Ravi Batra's popular book, *The Depression of 1990,* made this claim, and it is irrelevant. It would be a miracle if our capitalistic society did not accumulate wealth. A.C. Pigou, an economist at Oxford University, did a great deal of research on this topic and found that in all societies in all times the distribution of wealth remained the same within a narrow range— in other words, there have always been the rich and the poor. Historically, every panic in America since 1800 has been precipitated by the public's abuse of bank credit. Economists seem to understand much about credit, which they describe as "liquidity," and they add to our confusion because debt and its interest are mysteriously ignored by our experts. So, their advice now will not be worth much to those of us strangling on debts we are having trouble paying back.

Is a repudiation of Uncle Sam of his own debts possible? It could happen, but it is far too soon to tell. If so, that would be the time to head for the hills because we would see breakdown in our society at every level, and in every town. Lewis Mumford wrote in 1974, "We have entered a new Dark Age, but no one seems to know this."

We might very well be on the cutting edge now of an epochal transformation of our society. America could change dramatically and maybe never change back. This is because the institutions that supported the capitalistic economic system are in trouble now: education, law, medicine, banks, etc. If they are failing, then the industrial system itself is obviously failing. So, should we now prepare for a new and vastly different future for our country and for ourselves...a new mode of living...a new frontier? No one can know about this now, but we can heed growing warning signs and prepare ourselves for the worst...just in case. That only makes good sense.

Let me explain. A phenomena that mathematicians are familiar with but which most of us do not know is the idea of "rate of change." It means the degree of anything in relation to units of something else. So, when the rate of change increases, the growth of the units feed on themselves making future growth larger and faster. Thus, our GNP has for many years averaged 3% compounded and this gave us for a long time good economic times. When it falls to 2% compounded, then the slower growth feeds on itself worsening the entire economy. The rate of change in economic affairs alters our livelihoods in a remarkable manner.

Another example: when banks increase their lending, the rate of change in this loan process speeds up and more loans are made, and more credit is issued. Our economy is then given a large uplift in business activity since the vast credit extensions make business prosperous.

In late 1980, however, the amount of loans made by all American banks began to decline and the decline in a falling rate of change fed on itself and accelerated. Since lending is a bank's main business, it was reasonable to predict that if this decline continued the banks would have to shut down since no one would be borrowing. In addition, the slowdown in lending meant the disappearance of the American money supply because the money supply was borrowed money—debts and the other side, credits. For example, when you bought a car and financed it, you added credits to the system in the amount of our loan. When you paid off the loan, the credits disappeared and so did that amount of the money supply.

Furthermore, in 1990 something interesting was beginning to emerge in rate of changes: It was revealed in January 1990 that for the first time in U.S. history the federal government spent more money in 1989 on interest, $241 billion, than on Social Security, $229 billion.[4] It appeared harmless, but it was a nuclear financial bomb getting ready to detonate.

In this book I calculate that the total debt of the federal government is over $11 trillion dollars. This includes budget debts and off-budget debts, plus governmental guarantees and insurances. All of this debt naturally carries interest and it compounds. But, remember, compounded growth is exponential

growth; growing 2,4,8,16, doubling, and not growing arithmetically at a rate of 1,2,3,4, this compound growth is relentless and
unforgiving. Give compound interest enough time and it will
consume all borrowers as I point out.

At any rate, I speculate that our economic lives could get
much worse before they show any signs of getting better. If you
agree with a sense of the difficult-debt-repayment argument, I
provide ideas you can adopt as an individual to weather whatever financial storms erupt in this decade.

You probably wonder, "How can anything bad happen to me,
or to America?" In other words, where did all of the wealth we
created go?

Our wealth was built on the quicksands of credit and debt. As
we saw in 1989, an early signal and a major casualty of bad debts
was the crisis in the savings and loan industry—a problem so
enormous as to be almost an illusion. It was artfully manipulated
as a problem and the public was led to believe that it was
controlled. But it was not.

But the losses in thrift and real estate and leveraged buyouts
and in many other ways that were finally revealed to the public
had the overall and arching effect of literally making our credit-
wealth vanish. In addition, our credit system is leveraged: the
same reserves required under our fractional reserve banking
system mean that a bank creating $1 through a first loan can then
lend eight to ten times more, or $8 to $10. But, by the same
token, when the credit contracts, $10 must be called in to get the
original $1 you ask for at the bank. So, $10 is then destroyed to
retrieve $1. And this in essence is where all of the wealth has
gone: it was eaten up in bad losses which were leveraged.

Do not perceive this view to be overly gloomy, but sunny
optimism and silver linings do not of themselves insure a better
life. The plain evidence of thousands of years of history tells us
that people do not always do the right thing. Nations sometimes
go wrong. If the American public had listened more to the
gloomy naysayers, the American savings and loan industry would

not be in such bad shape; the junk bond market would not have swollen to such unsustainable proportions; there might be more ozone in the upper atmosphere and less oil in the oceans. History and experience tells us we need to hear gloomy voices and sometimes even be guided by them.

For example, warnings about the threat of a breakdown in America's infrastructure have gone unheeded for over ten years. In the *Los Angeles Times*, February 11, 1990, the headline said "California is falling apart, and it will take more than $65 billion to repair the roads, bridges, dams sewer and water systems, etc., all over the state."[5] It was previously estimated years ago the problem is also a national one, requiring over $1 trillion to do the repairs all over America. In America, however, spending for public works dropped from 2.3% of the Gross National Product to 1% during the last twenty years. Why? Well, infrastructure is most times literally out of sight, and out of sight often means out of mind, so funds were borrowed and spent for things the public could see and touch. Now the system is falling apart. To get the funds needed in California and in America means borrowing the funds, but that is the problem now: too much debt at every level, as noted.

EARLY WARNING SIGNS OF CRISIS

Back in 1981-82, the American economic system went through a huge credit crisis and, for a time, saw the highest interest rates in U.S. history when the Prime Rate touched 21-1/2% in 1981. And, as detailed in the book, high interest rates also have the perverse effect of destroying capital—if interest rates rise, bond prices fall, underlying collateral in loans lose value, and so on. Since a large percentage of assets of banks, pension funds, insurance companies, etc., is in holdings of government debts, mortgages, and other forms of debt, the effect of this episodic rise in rates was devastating: of the leading 32 life insurance companies, not a single one was liquid back then.[6]

For example, State Farm Life had a statutory surplus of $484.7 million at the end of 1980, but if they had marked their bonds and mortgages down to reflect the crisis and their true value, they would have had a deficit of $916.5 million. Prudential Life Insurance Company had a surplus of $2.8 billion, but if they had also marked their debts down to their new low values, their deficit would have been $13 billion. Metropolitan Life Insurance Company was in the same lifeboat: a surplus of $2 billion, but unrealized bond and mortgage losses of $14.2 billion. It was so bad in 1981 that U.S. Treasury Bonds traded at less than 58 cents on the dollar. If all of those debts held by others had been written down back then, "the entire credit system that underpins the economy would have collapsed."

Why did the economy not collapse back then? The high interest rates froze business activity resulting in the worst recession since the Great Depression. But (and this is important), back then it was still possible to "reliquify"—that is, borrow new credit dollars and use them to revitalize economic activity. This credit infusion saved the day—rates fell, bond prices rose, and the vast extra and continued borrowing by all sectors in America in the 1980s continued to perpetuate the illusion of prosperity. In the process of adding another one trillion in dead debt weight to a system on the brink, the system was saved for a time.

The argument of this book is that that was the last time the American financial system could be reliquified—the last time buyers could be found for any debt. Now we are sinking under the accumulated national monster debt load of over $20 trillion with its rising compound interest.... The lifeboats are now waterlogged and ready to sink. The system may no longer be savable.

RISING LEVERAGE—ANOTHER PROBLEM

Leverage is the use of debt instead of equity to raise funds, a familiar development in the American financial scene from 1982 to 1988, since it increased at an average annual rate of three percent, according to the Federal Reserve Bank of San Francisco. At the same time this was happening, the increase in interest payment obligations was four percent. This increase in interest obligations relative to cash flow meant a higher level of cash flow was needed to keep an organization solvent, and "poses an increased risk to the economy as a whole," according to that bank.

They concluded that the use of leverage was a "cause for concern," and it could "make an economy-wide credit squeeze a more serious threat."

That is the central message of this book: we have debt levels all over America that are all highly leveraged, carry high rates of interest and are, in general, unrepayable. And, too bad for us, the list of mammoth debtors now also includes the federal government. So, unlike previous crises in American history, the one we are now in has the strength to engulf Uncle Sam.

The book outlines the problem. If you agree with the argument, you can prepare for it. If you do not agree, you would not take steps anyway to safeguard your assets other than those you already believe in and are involved in.

FORWARD
REFERENCES

1. Naisbitt, John, Aburdene, Patricia, *Megatrends 2000* (Wm. Morrow & Co., N.Y.C., 1990).

2. *Los Angeles Times,* November 29, 1989.

3. *Los Angeles Times,* December 16, 1989.

4. *Barron's,* January 15, 1990.

5. *Los Angeles Times,* February 11, 1990.

6. *Wall Street Journal,* March 29, 1990.

CHAPTER ONE

THE FOUNTAIN OF ECONOMIC GROWTH

Americans have become conditioned to short-term views of all events that touch their economic lives. Because of this, long-term events have been ignored at virtually every level of our society, from Washington and Wall Street to Main Street. The long-term trends—secular—are hardly visible in everyday life, but they plod inexorably on building on their own achievements, year by year, and are hardly noticeable, but measured century by century are matters of great importance. We are now only beginning to learn this as our mountain of debts loom as insurmountable terrain.

Our present super-debt-crisis, which refuses to go away, is the most sinister, as though it cannot show its face. It is not so much a hurricane as a flood with the water now rising alarmingly, under a sky obstinately grey and waterlogged. All the foundations of economic life and all of the lessons of our national experience past and present are now being challenged. We must, then, look back to find out why we enjoyed such phenomenal economic growth and why our economic growth is now coming to an end—never to return.

In the *Wealth of Nations* in 1776, Adam Smith wrote that two of the epochal discoveries in all recorded history were the discovery of America and the passage to the East Indies by the Cape of Good Hope. He believed these to be the two greatest events recorded in the history of populations.

This vast unexploited territory—the New World—was there for the taking. Economists say that there is no such thing as a "free lunch," but this discovery of America proved that there is, indeed, a free lunch. Here was a giant treasure ready to be exploited (pirated is a better word). And so it was.

We have been taught to believe that America grew because we work harder, the market place determines our actions and sets our guidelines, and, above all, it is our destiny as Americans. But the fact that all of the wealth was there for the taking—free and ready for us to rip off—was somehow ignored. Woe unto us because, like all good things, resources are finite, not infinite. We are only now discovering this truth.

Western Europe was—around 1500 when capitalism started— virtually static. It had an area of approximately 3,000,000 miles and a population of 150,000,000. And that was it. Decade after decade. The carrying capacity of the day-to-day world known by the average person living in Western Europe had been reached.

"Economic Growth" and "Progress"—the ideas that we value so highly today—would have baffled medieval Europe's typical citizen. There were very few entrepreneurs back then (as there may be in America's future) because there was almost no wealth to manipulate. Opportunities for the accumulation of excess capital, the investment of such funds, or the drawing of interest on them were so sparse that public banking was completely unknown, and private banks were few, far between, and used only by a handful of popes, monarchs, and emperors.

Just staying alive was a major accomplishment in Europe during the Middle Ages. The continent's population was static because it had reached a semi-starvation subsistence balance on the land it inhabited. There wasn't really enough food to go around. Its citizens lived in a mean, brutish, closed little world. Death—with its possibility of Heaven—offered most inhabitants of the continent their only hope of escape. (When the world credit system dies in 1989 and 1990, people on all continents may find their living standards going back to that Medieval brutish period.)

Then, suddenly, within the merest blink of time as the planet measures its age, Europe was buried under an absolute avalanche of riches. In a twinkling, the land available to its people was increased five times over by the "discovery" of and claims made upon North America, South America, South Africa, Australia, New Zealand, and hundreds of islands in oceans barely known before.

Thanks to the plundering of these new (to them) lands, the amount of gold and silver handled by the inhabitants of Europe was multiplied 15 times over. The grains, fibers, timber, furs, base metals, and many other material goods—such as chocolate, rubber, corn, pumpkins, quinine, tobacco, potatoes, buffalo robes, and kangaroo pelts—further surprised, delighted, and enriched them.

The boom was on, and it lasted in round numbers from 1500 to 1970. Four hundred and seventy years. Four and three quarter centuries in which all the inhabitants of the Western world—and especially those of us lucky enough to live in one part or another of the Mother Lode itself—were caught up in this overpowering flash flood of new wealth and swept into a hitherto unknown appreciation of the individual—self-motivation, capitalism, and democracy all took new meanings.

You cannot develop a work ethic when there is not enough work—or wages, or even food—to go around. It is extremely easy, on the other hand, to "discover" the virtues of hard work when—on every side—you see people getting rich exactly in proportion to the amount of time and energy they invest in claiming previously unclaimed land, furs, food, and seemingly limitless quantities of other real wealth

When more land than can possibly be farmed, more gold then can be counted, and more "work" than people to do (in the form of grabbing a share of an apparently endless bounty) is spread before a group of people (our ancestors), and you may find that all of our most cherished concepts—"freedom," "independence," individualism," "self reliance," "courage," "initiative," "invention," and "industry"—nearly discover themselves.

If this only had been able to go on forever, instead of just long enough (470 years) to make us think that such a one-time explosion of windfall wealth is the natural way of the world. Which it is not, of course. The flood of "found" riches crested in 1970. The tidal wave which picked us up and washed us to our high-water mark—our elevated (in every sense of the word) "standard of living"—is receding. For many Americans this started in the early 1970s when real wages started to decline, and, later, for the farmer when his product prices started falling and when he started going deeper in debt to survive financially.

There's no more free land for millions of pioneers to homestead, no more buffalo herds to slaughter, no more fifty-pound nuggets of copper lying on the ground in Michigan, and no more unclaimed wealth in North America, South America, Australia, New Zealand, or South Africa. The Mother Lode, for all practical purposes, has been completely mapped and tapped. There is nothing left for us now. Nothing.

It has been believed and taught to generations of Americans that new technology will create still another new frontier—genetic engineering, robotics, and miracle health cures—which will, we believe, turn the future around and make the path of the past born again.

It is a historical fact that only new found land and riches can add to the sum total of things in the absolute. Technology can do nothing but change the form of what is already there. Certainly the skill with which science has performed this function has misled us into the assumption that science can contribute to mankind unlimited benefits without regard for substance. But this is a false assumption and appears as such when we look at the whole picture. We all believe that our time is a unique "high-tech society," which may constantly uplift our living standards without end. We emphasize mathematics and science education in our schools and we want our children to become engineers and scientists so they can carry on this "illusion."

To put it differently: long before massive oil spills, Chernobyl, and microwave cooking...long before smog, pesticides, industrial pollution, and other contamination began killing tens of thousands of people annually, we should have understood that science really creates nothing. It only speeds up the destruction of what is already there.

Which would you rather have now, the earth as it was in 1500—before the Age of Science—with its natural forests, clear streams and lakes, virgin soils, and precious metals intact? Or the earth as it is now, today...covered with stumps, foul streams, eroded soils, and depleted energy and metal resources? Technology has given us the luxuries and comforts in a glorious holiday in which we eat and breed, but all the time it is swinging off the limb on which it complacently sits, and on which our civilization rests.

Nor should we be misled by the "there's always more where that came from" philosophy which dominated our oil and gas— and many other—industries since World War II. There is not more.

The years ahead may be far different from what we have known since the turn of the century. Our most cherished institutions, myths, illusions, and ways of doing business may soon be discarded in the cataclysmic changes now on the horizon. Our future may be one of *upheaval*—and long-term change.

We are heading towards a process of devolution and retrogression instead of evolution and progress. Rural life may become more important, and cities may become less pleasant places (as many already have) in which to live. Population is stabilizing in some industrialized countries and is headed towards the steady-state characteristics of the Medieval Age. What contributed to this? It was mostly due to the death of the global credit system, the end of the debt age, then starting anew. New money systems and new ways of living are bound to follow.

In this massive upheaval, the democracy carried over from

the Mother-Lode may give way to a totalitarian state for awhile—
in America, at least. The political power may be centralized by a
dictator and individuals may become less important than they
already are. Capitalism is on the decline and its expensive prosperity is now a memory—ready for the history books.

Population must, and will, come to its final balance with the
land—food and clothing and life's basics may cost more tomorrow than they did yesterday. Because of this, we may give up our
efforts to feed the world's hungry, defend the "free" world, and
work to prop up our own economy and the economies of others
that are in the same lifeboat with us.

THE AGE OF THE MOTHER-LODE

Historians of tomorrow will view the discovery of America
in 1492 as an aberration in the long sweep of human endeavor
and history, a temporary departure from the normal in the long
spans of mankind over the ages. It was a strange historical detour
in which Americans, and other industrial-capitalist countries,
developed all sorts of quaint ideas about property for all, freedom
for all, and continuous growth.

The Institutions that we now take for granted may, tomorrow,
seem to us to have been so specialized that they could not
survive the return of society to a normal state, where there was a
balance between land and men who live on it.

Our politicians and our economists, and just plain mainstream Americans, will find it hard to believe that almost 500
years of prosperity, with its ups and downs, began to draw to a
close in the early 1970s, and now, in the 1990s, is ending. We
will not think that this long prosperity *was due entirely* to the
windfall riches of North America and South America that we
have been plundering for the past 500 years.

They may also find out that prosperity is not created by
manipulating interest rates, the establishment of social security
systems and welfare programs, or any other shuffling of eco-

nomic theories, political platforms, or social schemes. These have mainly been just old fashioned smoke and mirrors.

We were all poor once; suddenly, one day, we got rich. And we stayed rich until 1970 when we all started to get poor again. Slowly and hardly noticeably, the reality of this poverty was hidden until 1990 by a final gushing of the American credit-money well just before it ran dry. We borrowed to finance our way of life and we got used to living on credit, and then the credit stream dried up.

Overnight we started becoming poor again. Many still believe that if we can tinker a little more, if the government can do "something," then the credit spigot may be turned on again, and the good times will roll out again. But the ebb and flow of financial affairs could not be controlled by Washington—their attempts to preserve the old economy are illusory and ill-fated, doomed to fail.

Lots of luck. Unless another unmapped and untapped planet swings so closely into the orbit of the earth that we can build a bridge across and start plundering virgin territory once again, the past good times we all so fondly remember may be gone for good. And with it may go all of our quaint, social, economic, and political theories, as well.

Which now leaves us with still more of the long, slow slide that all of our institutions have been struggling with since at least the early 1970s when the oil crisis emerged. This was followed by the farm crisis of the late 1970s, and then the breakdown of the financial superstructure commencing with the beginning of the Savings and Loan problems in 1980-82, when interest rates soared, and began their destruction. Then there followed the virtual total breakdown of that system in the late 1980s.

DISMAL OUTLOOK

From now on—for as long as you, your children, and your children's children live—we can expect the overall quality of life, as we have come to know it, to do nothing but decline. There will, naturally, be ups and downs along the way. But, in general, each and every year from now on will likely be a little worse than the one before.

There may be less and less food to go around; this may have started with the U.S. and the world drought that started in 1988. Fewer clothes and materials of every kind may be around. Average life spans may decrease, not increase as they did during the prosperous times.

There may *not* be a government in Washington as we now know it. The troubled times will bring us—out of somewhere— a Napoleon-like figure in order to try to give the public what it reveres most: *personal security.*

Nothing will run tomorrow as well as it used to yesterday. There may be growing attempts to secede from old political and geographical organizations; the new dictator may put an end to cries for "action." There may be power outages and computer breakdowns which will cripple our credit-money and social welfare systems. Telephone services may be irregular, roads may fall apart. Many of the physical, social, and economic interconnections that hold industrial society may be severed. Lawlessness may be dealt with by the dictator.

That is the trend ahead—a long, slow, and bitter downward slide. And the bad news is that at any given time there will always exist an increasingly great chance for an unexpected savage catastrophe of truly terrifying proportions, size, shape, and hue.

But be of good cheer. The message and lesson of this book is to give a broad view of what is *really* going on in America and the world. We will survive this coming disaster, as we have before, but this time by going backwards and amassing and working with the useful arts and crafts widely used before 1900 in small, decentralized, self-contained, defensible agrarian communities—which centuries ago were called "monasteries" and "walled cities."

CHAPTER TWO

SOCIAL/BUSINESS COSTS, CHANGING LIFESTYLES

During most of our lives, when we are taught about how to run any type of business, there is no accounting for the many invisible costs of conducting a business. Some of these costs include auto pollution, chemical assaults from detergents, deforestation, etc. They go on and add up. But, as consumers, we are so far removed from the production process that we do not think of this as a "cost" and ignore it until we are forced to confront and deal with it, like now.

The pollution of the earth has brought enormous social costs and public hostility. Chemicals have become such an indispensable part of modern life that it is hard to find a product that does not contain them, has been processed with them, or is wrapped in them. It has been estimated that since the 1950s, the chemical industry worldwide has increased its yearly production of bulk chemicals (from plastics to antifreeze) from two million tons to nearly 100 million tons.[1] Most of those chemicals are still around, in some shape or form, lingering and polluting long after their original job is done.

More and more the public thinks—properly—of the chemical industry as the center of hazardous waste, toxic spills, plastic litter, the destruction of forests, dead seals, and mountains of diapers. Consumers shift from one product to another searching for the one that is least hazardous. While they are doing this, still more dangerous chemicals are being hatched.

But we have been misled, too. The theories explaining how our production system works had a tendency to conceal rather than open up the doors to these costs. Our economists searched for the growth touchstone, but their ideas and economic theories were irrelevant since they ignored an environment that would be compatible with the requirements for human health, well being, and survival.

For over a century, these long-neglected problems and hard facts have been cited by critics and dissenters from mainstream thought in economics, but ignored. For example, K. William Kapp wrote, "The long term implications of ignoring these complications may well turn out to be as far-reaching as some of the problems raised by nineteenth century social reformers and socialist critics who concentrated their attention on exploitation, poverty and economic instability. Ultimately, the disruption of man's environment may reveal itself our most crucial problem …and will call for a radical change of the present institutionalized system of investment and decision making by private firms and public agencies with regard to the choice of investment and as production patterns."[2] This was written in 1950!

Now as we near the turn of the century, we are waking up to the reality of this accurate, but ignored, prophecy.

Unemployment, as an example, is an overhead cost that businesses shift to you and me when they lay us off, and they are then reluctant to contribute to our unemployment pay. This is now realized by those in the ranks of the unemployed.

We cannot continue these social costs, which encompass far more than pollution and unemployment. These are only the closest to our present problems. It forces us now to make some tough choices. We must shift "down" industrial production and the investment that goes into it because of growing social costs. The smaller population and productions downshifts will change our future work styles. We could then, over time:

1) Live close to home.
2) Work in small businesses.
3) Less travel by all of our society.

But it may be several generations before the earth is clear again of the damage industrial society has done. And we will all be a part of this unique and unusual clean-up.

Social costs and their settlement is just another face of the giant transformation our society is now undergoing. It will be years before the necessary changes are done, but they may be now in motion and they are irreversible.

Besides social costs and industrial giantism vanishing, we may see major political changes and social changes, as well. When we look back, it will seem amazing that we lived as we did since World War II. In the long range of history it could appear as a blip on a radar screen, no more.

A PUBLIC OUT OF WORK

It is interesting that in America so few people have the time or the interest to try and find out why some people seem to get so rich and why most people are at an average-middle or low wage level.

The history of this spread in wages between the rich and poor goes back in U.S. history to about the beginning, when America was a "pre-industrial country." It was a time we all remember seeing depicted on Western movies when the lives of most people were lived in a local community. Each community was, to a large extent, self-contained, and its contacts with the outside world were infrequent. These have been described as "island communities." Each town had its local elite—its merchants, bankers, clergymen, attorneys, physicians, editors, and so forth— to whom the community looked to for leadership. These elites, of course, enjoyed their status. But the existence of this small knit community with a shared set of values was also beneficial to other groups in the community. Historians have observed that nineteenth century workers were often able to use these shared values to gain community support for fair treatment for themselves and their friends.

But the rapid industrialization of the United States during the late nineteenth century (the Industrial Revolution) upset this placid and small world. The development of national systems of transportation and communications, highly concentrated and powerful industrial and financial systems, mass circulations of newspapers and magazines, along with the growth of cities (that big industry nurtured) submerged the independence of the nation's separate local towns. The small personal community was replaced by a large, anonymous society in which the importance of one's place and achievements in the local context were nearly dissolved.

As a general rule, the division of work, in large or small communities, led to a growing spread in incomes. Some got high wages and others low wages. This has been true not only in America but in all societies, and the distribution of income has remained the same, within a narrow range, all through time. There have always been the rich and the poor—everywhere—all through economic history.

When we move into a period of hard times, like now, Americans historically have moved backwards towards community-oriented values simply because so many are again in need. With perhaps 35% of all workers now unemployed, more without a regular source of income, and still more in fear that they are going to lose their jobs, most people quickly realize they face a common predicament. The 1980 ideas of self indulgence and "going it alone," and the so-called "free market" (an integral part of the failing capitalistic system) with no thought of how it impacts others vanishes. Fast. The egotism and vanity of recent years gives way to compassion.

The quest for justice in the Great Depression implied no desire to destroy the individual or to impose totalitarian collectivism. It merely meant that more people sought a greater degree of sharing, a more ethical and cooperative individualism. No more dog-eat-dog lifestyle. But it occurred not necessarily in obliteration of the self, but a recognition of the rights, needs, and humanity of others. Franklin Roosevelt said it well in a speech in 1936, "I believe in individualism...up to the point where the individual starts to operate at the expense of the community."

John Steinbeck, back in the 1930s, stated this emerging social quality beautifully: "The baby has a cold. Here, take this blanket. It's wool. It was my mother's blanket—take it for the baby. This is the thing to bomb. This is the beginning—from 'I' to 'We.'" Steinbeck went to the heart of the economic influence on the change in values for prosperity to depression: "For the quality of owning freezes you forever into 'I,' and cuts you off forever from the 'We.'" And this is where we have all been since World War II—in a society dominated by money. We have thought of nothing else...until now.

Like all Depressions, the coming impact of this one may be devastating for most of us. To repeat, the public quickly rejects the "acquisitive individualism"—"free market ideas"—associated with the business ethic of the 70s and 80s, but it is not easy for the public to see what might replace it. Self-blame was a natural outgrowth for the self-congratulation of the preceding period of prosperity.

We have yet to reach the turning point where *hope* again re-emerges. It is a necessary ingredient in any significant movement for change. The return to the old values of a competitive, acquisitive, greedy society are now very far away and, it seems to me, they will probably never return in our lifetimes.

What is happening is a return to the older values of justice, cooperation, and moral economics. They are being reshaped now, but they will, or already have, give us a new cooperative approach, one with no roots in the former free-marketplace economy.

The current economic and mood shifts of the public are far from absolute but, as a rule of thumb, working class people have always been more likely to hold values centered on cooperation, sharing, equity, fairness, and justice than have their affluent countrymen. The latter have, throughout our history, been more likely to defend the marketplace as the sole determinant of the distribution of income the economy can create. The poor—whether farmers or service workers—have generally been less willing worshipers at the shrine of Adam Smith, who believed the common good would be served by competition.

So far as the public was concerned, as long as a marketplace economy provided a reasonable chance for them to work, they were more likely to accept it. But during the present hard times, when the maldistribution of income is so evident, the working man naturally turns to the community or to the Federal government for action to implement—or counteract—the marketplace. Most working people believe that morality ought to have a role in the workings of the economy. The Wall Street cheating scandals in the late 1980s was a profound shock to the average man in the way he thought about how economic and financial affairs should be conducted in America.

The basic reason for this difference is not hard to find. The self-interest of the have-nots is better served by a more equitable distribution of income, whereas the self-interest of the wealthy is obviously served by keeping things as they are. This in no sense makes the two positions ethically equivalent. The self-interest of the poor coincides with justice; that of the rich, with injustice. The meaning of this, as in all previous Depressions, leads the lower and middle classes to demand government action to help them. Workers and farmers had many similar protests in the 1870s, 1890s, and 1930s. One key difference now from the last Great Depression is that we are long overdue for the swing to more humanitarianism. This Depression could also be deeper, wider, and may last much longer than Great Depression I. In addition, this Depression could impact a far larger segment of middle-class America. For the first time, middle-class America will be hard hit and will come to identify its interests with those of the poor, whom they had long ignored for many reasons. The combination of all these ingredients will make values of compassion, sharing, and justice be more dominant than they have been before in our history.

Up until now, each Depression in the U.S. has been worse than the one preceding it, and now we are headed towards the very worst of all. Why must the coming Depression be so terrible? So severe? So unrelenting? Perhaps the most important reason is one that surfaced in the 1930s: as the U.S. became less agrarian and more industrial, less rural and more urban, an increasing percentage of the American population became susceptible to the ups-and-downs of a market economy. Stated simply: more and more people became dependent as the nation industrialized and as the urban working class people who rented their apartments and whose income was entirely derived from wages and salaries found themselves in very desperate straits when they lost their jobs, as millions did, and could find no other employment.

Depressions leave massive unemployment and this always starts protest. Worker's optimism turns rapidly into pessimism and they become angry, ready to undertake any kind of action—even radical—to help their cause.

In past depressions these events alarmed middle-class Americans, some of whom believed revolution might be imminent, particularly since many sectors—like farmers—were seething with populism. In the past, middle class America cast its lot with business and dug into it to defend economic orthodoxy and the status quo.

This time, however, it may be very different. Middle Americans will be caught up in the powerful economic decline and find themselves trapped in debts they are unable to pay. They will learn fast that the past "good life" was built on quicksand. Overnight, they may join the poor. They will be furious and demand change. Unemployed people are restless and dangerous, as we will find out.

And, differently this time, too, is that the Federal Government will be less able than ever before to effect social and economic planning because its own creditworthiness will become suspect. The alarming impact this event could have on all of our lives may portend greater change than most people can now imagine.

We will soon see violent economic shifts, which will light a fire under our social, political, and cultural systems and change them too. An epic transformation is underway.

THE RISE OF THE SERVICE SOCIETY

The Labor Department reported in the *Los Angeles Times* on January 7, 1989, that of the non-farmer workers in America, 76% were employed in service work. How did America become transformed from an industrial society to a service society?

As the standard of living of Americans began to rise after World War II, propelled initially by war savings and later by credit, Americans had enough income left over to buy consumer goods beyond bare necessities. Production shifted to more upscale consumer products, including VCR's, stereos, and so on.

The rise in real income for the average worker continued until 1973, when it turned down. And when it turned down, consumers, to support their newly acquired luxury habits, began to overuse credit, which lenders made easy as pie to get. This rapidly produced $11 trillion in domestic debt, $9 trillion in the private sector.

BROAD CHANGE

The protests which erupted in 1968 over the war in Vietnam by the young generation first, and then other sectors of the population, marked the break with the familiar American past— the one we read about in history books, the one with two political parties, the one with large corporations making steel and mining for iron.

All of a sudden millions of young Americans changed their hair styles, their dress codes, their moral habits, and their views about the way things were. At first this broad change was perceived to be an aberration and, later, that the new generation would simply—given time—fit back into the old mold of our historical past. That did not prove to be the case.

Because this generation had also been impacted by television (the first), it led, among other things, to the breakdown of education and the rapid growth of functional illiteracy in the public.

These changes were symptomatic of an even deeper change: in front of us, the institutions of capitalism seemed to be falling apart, and patching them together seemed all but impossible. The post office did not work, the defense department could not defend, the government could not balance its budgets, one-third of the public had no medical insurance, the public lost interest in voting, and public officials lost interest in the public, etc.

All of a sudden it seemed to us that we moved to "living in the fast lane" (that is what this way of life was called), wildly and electronically, and this change took with it many of the old American verities of honesty, faith, dependability, and "knowing." And so our world changed. The old values were pushed aside. But now the stage is being set for them to return to our lives, so we are simply closing the circle as so often happens in history.

BIGNESS AND SMALLNESS

The old economic wisdom that bigger is better brought its toll. The public employed by bigger companies were summarily let out of work and learned, rapidly, that being bigger was not better, especially if you did not have a paycheck.

This will set the stage for a migration from cities to beyond the suburbs—back to the country, where new small communities will form and smallness will replace bigness. This is a certainty because the long years of expansion are being replaced by long years of contraction, meaning a lower standard of living and a simpler way of life. But, and more importantly, it will be back in the community that work can be found for the masses of unemployed.

The ability of the government, or the large corporations, to solve unemployment problems this time around will not succeed any more in our time than it did in the 1930s when, in 1938, the unemployment figures were still over ten million. The New Deal did not solve unemployment. And until we solve unemployment, we cannot solve anything else. It is work that is in our hearts and souls and not handouts in public service jobs, cleaning streets, waiting for unemployment checks, and other old-fashioned solutions. This is to be the central problem for America and other nations in the 1990s and the turn of the century. Everything else will pale by comparison.

For readers of this book, a job is the Number One problem. And a creative and meaningful job is needed, not make-work.

Once we solve that riddle we may get our society back on track again. We can then face the challenges of the next century.

UNEMPLOYMENT

Back in the 1930s unemployment rose to around 28 million—about 30 percent of the people were thrown out of work.

This time it is bound to be worse. The manufacturing sector is shutting down, and millions will be thrown out of work there. The highly touted service economy will also retreat since it is parasitical in nature—living off the wealth created elsewhere. Although politicians worked feverishly all through the 1980s to create jobs, the jobs were mostly unskilled and dead-end. And the bulk of them were created in small businesses and not by the large and powerful corporations.

But rising unemployment levels will cause Americans, at many levels, to move backwards in their lifestyles and toward community-oriented values. This will happen because so many will be in need—food shortages, empty supermarkets, transportation breakdowns, etc. People will quickly realize they have a common predicament—the free market, going it alone and getting a job will be gone. The egotism and vanity of that time will give way to compassion. In the last Great Depression the public sought a greater degree of sharing, a more ethical and cooperative individualism. They will again.

But the marketplace and democracy may be ending. History could happen again and a "man on a white horse" could come to power. Who can know now?

Hidden away in our collective lives, we value "security" above all else. Security at home, in the workplace, wherever: security. We ignore its crucial value until we have to face its loss. And, most of all, *financial security*—without money, we do not eat.

Now, with vast social discontent created by millions of unemployed, and with a government in Washington powerless to help because of its own financial problems, the public will turn to a charismatic leader. "It can't happen in America," you think. That is dead wrong. Food shortages alone will cause desperate people to do desperate things. The old order will be gone. Old rules will be gone. We will be living, briefly, through a period of lawlessness. Courts will be closed, the institution that supported our old order will be in disarray: health care, police systems, distribution systems, money systems, and so on. Out of this chaos there will be an enormous demand for "Order!"

History brought societies to the end of the Age of Religion. Now, the Age of Politics that capitalism spawned is also ending. We will live tomorrow in an Age of Tyranny. Maybe as St. Thomas Aquinas said, we will be lucky enough to be ruled by a "beneficent dictator."

"Why must this happen," you think? The good times are gone. Depressions are devastating for everyone. The public rejects promptly the ethic of "acquisitive individualism and free markets" and reaches a vital turning point: surviving in an increasingly hostile environment.

The old values of competition, acquisitiveness and human greed will be gone. They will be replaced by *fear.* Fear will bring cooperation and a moral form of economics. To repeat, all through history working class people have always been more likely to hold values centered on cooperation, sharing, equity, fairness and justice more than their affluent counterparts have. The affluent always defend the marketplace as the sole determinant of income.

As long as the market economy provided a reasonable chance for the public to work, they accepted it. But now we are in a growing period of hard times. The maldistribution of income is more present, the working man turns to outside help for help. But this is not a replay of the 1930s when we had a financially sturdy government ready to lend us funds to get our lives going again. Instead, we are frozen into this time when the Government itself is insolvent—it cannot help, and the marketplace ruling our affairs will become history very quickly.

The basic reason for all of this is not hard to find.

TOMORROW'S WORK

We believe that we need a city because culture cannot rise out of farming. There has always had to be a sort of critical density formed to produce the flowering of the human spirit. Cities have existed for five thousand years, but they never grew huge until the recent past. Why was this? A big city does not live on itself—it lives off the land. A city in the inland lives off the circle of land around it for its provisions. In the far distant past that circle could not be very far away because the only transport energy was animal and man. Cities near the sea could and did use other transport energy—wind power, for example—and could be provisioned by ships. So until three hundred years ago, there were no cities larger than, say, 300,000 people.

This bottleneck on the ultimate city-size was broken by the

exploitation of fossil fuels—first coal, then oil, and developing transport technology to use them so that big cities could be provisioned with energy from all over the world. But there is also a limit to the growth of cities: if, for example, it took in the historical past 80 people to feed 100, then 80 percent of the people had to stay on the land and only 20 percent were able to live in the cities. But if, as we had in America, there was a tremendous increase in farm productivity, five people can then feed 100. This allows 95 percent of the people to then live in cities and only five percent had to stay on the farm (which they are now, in fact). So, beyond fossil fuels, it took enormous increases in productivity per man in agriculture, and this made the city possible. But it also brought an alarming use of chemicals by farmers—and that presented another problem. It is not possible to live without trade-offs in any society.

THE FREE LUNCH

But for many years in America we have ignored the costs of any endeavor. We were told we land men on the moon and it would bring society huge benefits. We got to the moon, but the benefits, except for small ones, have yet to appear. We wanted better health care for our aging population, but no one wants to pay for it—least of all the rich who could afford it.

Cities are huge machines and require a constant input of energy. If we now face energy breakdowns, power outages and a demolished infrastructure in many cities, then people will leave the cities and want to work and make a living outside the city. What economic systems can they escape to? They can drop out of the cities, but they can't drop back into the farms like they did in the 1930s. So what can they drop into?

Our unemployment problem is one result of large-scale production and the large capital this took—that was capitalism. But capitalism is ending, so what will take the place of large-scale, highly complex and highly capital-intensive production?

If we went back a little and used small units, everything would not be so complex. We could train our engineers to use low-tech, simplified technology (instead of high-tech) which would take less capital. But you say, "That can't be done." We need our behemoth factories who make our toilet tissue and razor blades! But do we if those industries cannot provide jobs for most of the people most of the time?

We need real work, not make-work, and not public works projects like the New Deal created. But this means changing our lifestyles. And that is what we will all be doing as we transform from capitalism to a new society.

We have been brainwashed by high-tech and the idea that "bigger is better." But look what this has brought us: economic devastation. We now have the know-how to make things small again for most things—not airplanes and trucks, but for the things we all really need to survive on, and that takes less capital and will provide jobs.

The technological trend since World War II we think will promise a better life, but that was in the old capitalistic mode. But one promise this old technology did keep was to make jobs hard to find: robotizing and automated machines take the place of people. Instead, the people found work making hamburgers. Now we need real jobs for real people, now displaced by soaring unemployment so typical of all depressions in America since 1800. The capitalistic system barely changed with this perpetual booms and bust cycles—until now. Now it is being totally transformed.

Finding work alone demands vast political change.

The higher the tech, the more the public is excluded, the more complex it all is, and the more capital it takes. But people still put a high value on work.

It is possible tomorrow to have, in place of three auto plants, 300 small plants scattered all over America; to make cereals in 300 places where the resources are instead of three where the raw materials are expensively shipped to, and so on.

We can do this in America. We must do this if we are to provide meaningful work and allay social unrest which bursts out when men and women cannot find work.

REBEL AMERICA

The chief function of any economic system should be to provide a livelihood for the whole population. To survive, any system must take care of most of the people most of the time. If the government fails to do this, then it will be displaced, if not by a better, at least a different, order.

Most of the capitalistic systems in the world are pretty much alike: big cities, vast financial markets, vast systems to distribute the necessities of living, and so on.

When, however, something important happens to the public by a dramatic economic event, then everything that seemed familiar changes rather quickly. This process of change in America started perhaps as far back as 1970.

Now we have a world again may be entering another depression and large sections of the public may be deprived of their income for a prolonged period of time. This deprivation of income has led to upheaval in America in its past. Just going back to the 1930s, for example, we had farm milk strikes, violent farm mortgage foreclosures, etc. We realized, briefly, that even the most conservative and patriotic elements in the country could turn into revolutionaries. They demanded relief back then and they got it.

This is not meant to condemn or praise this force of action. But the point is that under conditions of dire necessity, it may be necessary to try to nationalize a large section of our economic life.

Under the capitalist economic system, just over three hundred years old, the world has grown richer in material goods. We have more of everything. And it is during this time that the most serious threats to our economic order have appeared.

There has been a drift for years in many countries towards what is called "state-capitalism." This is a system where the economic power, instead of remaining in the hands of private individuals, passes more and more completely into the hands of government. This has happened in many countries the world over.

LOOKING BACK

Over long time spans in United States history, and earlier history in other countries, there is a close relationship between the emergence of radical movements and economic depression. Hard times change many values at their roots: thus the reverence for money loses its power since the chance to acquire it virtually vanishes.

In U.S. history as early as 1786, Shay's Rebellion provided a dramatic warning to the Founding Fathers that those who bear the brunt of economic downgrading in the way they are forced to live will not remain passive. During the depression which began in 1828, the mere beginning of a labor movement in an almost purely agricultural country made their appearance with demands of a degree of radicalism hitherto unheard of on this side of the Atlantic. Boldly a ten-hour day, free schools, and abolition of imprisonment for debt were asked for.

Two great periods of radical reform movements emerged from 1837 to 1850 and from 1873 to 1896.

The first of these periods, which also coincides with the beginnings of the great evangelistic era, was especially characterized by utopian and humanitarian protests which took the form of model communities. In it Brook Farm, Fourier Phalanxes (twenty-nine in number), Fruitlands, and Hopedale made their appearance together with Skaneateles, Oneida, and the French Icanarian Communities.

During the 1840s the free soil movement arose. William Graham Sumner spoke of 1843 as the worst year in American history, and it was the following year that one of the first labor newspapers, the *Working Man's Advocate*, was revived, and the New England Workingmen's Association was also formed. In 1945, labor mass meetings were held in Boston, New York, and Pittsburgh. The years 1847 to 1849, after a decade of depression, were declared by Symes and Clements in the *Rebel America 1* to have been a "high tide of radical idealism." During this period, may Industrial Conferences were held by labor, and the National Reform Association was organized in an attempt to unite reform and labor movements.

Symes and Clements further commented: "With the early 1850s prosperity returned, and radicalism and humanitarianism again ran into discard."

The second great period of radical reform movements coincided with the long period of falling prices that began with the panic of 1873, and did not end until 1896. It was a period of general business and agricultural depression interrupted only occasionally, and for short periods of time, by mild recovery movements. Starting eight years after the Civil War, it holds the length-record for depressions in the United States—until now. All sorts of fantastic as well as intelligent reform movements made their appearance.

Especially bitter were the attacks on the railroads and on monopolies. An active farmer's movement emerged in the Central and Northwestern States. (Remember, the farmers had large political clout then, and their modern counterpart is the average worker in production or services, i.e., the consuming masses.)

In 1873 there was an unsuccessful attempt to form an independent Greenback Labor Party. In 1876 the Independent National (Greenback) Party, a farm movement, appeared. After the suppression of the great strikes of July 1877, labor united with it to form the National Party in 1879. Greenbackism, free silver, government money, and inflation were agitated with almost as much force as during the 1930s Depression. The new National Party condemned legislation in favor of money-lenders, bankers, and bondholders. It further condemned limiting the legal tender of Greenbacks, changing currency bonds into coin bonds, demonetizing silver, exempting government bonds from taxation, and contracting the currency medium. It fought forced resumption of specie payments, and the prodigal waste of public land. Still further—and even more boldly—some of its adherents advocated compulsory free education and no child labor under the age of fourteen. It was during this period, too, that the Popular movement began and became politically important.

H.R. Bruce wrote in *American Policies and Politics,* "Ever since the days of the Populists the farmers have swung to independent action in 'hard times.' When prices for farm products fall, when farm mortgages and farm debts rise and misfortune fastens itself upon the great agrarian regions, then a militant spirit arises to demand action from the government by the direct action of the farmers' own organizations and representatives."[3] Just as aptly, he might have added that if times are sufficiently hard, all other groups with political power will do the same thing. This is the way the American people can be expected to react. As long as they have some kind of financial security in their everyday lives, they will complacently go along, but if their financial security vanishes quickly, then expect this to bring demand for change of an episodic nature.

DEPRESSION AND RADICALISM

Some may doubt the connection between depression and the growth of radical movements, but you need only to go back to the period between 1933-36 for proof. Those were the days of the Father Coughlins, the Doctor Townsends, the Technocrats, the Huey Longs and many others with economic programs which many called the "lunatic fringe." Believe it or not, the more absurd the program, the more serious it was believed by large sections of the American public.

If, then, we are to avoid the drift towards state capitalism or some other new form of government which carries with it the loss of private initiative, of freedom of speech, and of checking individual liberties, long periods of economic depression must be avoided. But that has never been possible.

That is the point. We cannot eliminate periods of depression, and the one we are now in is on a scale perhaps unprecedented in its scope in all of economic history. It is world-wide and deep.

It is easy, believe it or not, for democracy to slip away and pass into the hands of a tyrant. When economic conditions turn sour, the process is accelerated and all but inevitable.

When the financial institutions that hold our collective monies are shut down, we will demand action. If they are not reopened promptly, such refusal could mean revolution.

VIOLENCE: THE CRISIS OF CONFIDENCE

We should take a sobering look at our native historical violence in order to understand better that our present Rebellious America is going to turn rapidly into Violent America.

Our bureaucratic institutions over the years have grown unresponsive and oftentimes uncontrollable. At the local level there are areas in cities today so violent that few local gang members will walk down them at night, and residents stay in locked homes. This is neither an exaggerated nor an isolated phenomena of our recent past.

Is all of this because we as a nation have failed to commit ourselves to social reform? Because we have failed to eliminate the injustices and inequalities which have fostered this surge of crime and civil strife, whose causes are as complex and varied as the answers of those who think they can halt it?

Historian Henry Steele Commanger demonstrated that our nation was not only born in violence, but steeped in a tradition of violence that has been "clad in the vestments of respectability and armored with the authority of the law."

Dr. Howard Zinn, a professor of government at Boston University, gave an example of the dichotomy in "justice." He wrote, "All you have to read is the Soledad letters of George Jackson, who was sentenced to one year to life of which he spent ten years, for a $70 robbery of a filling station. And then there is the U.S. Senator who is alleged to keep $185,000 a year, or something like that, on an oil depletion allowance. One is theft; the other is legislation."

This is no isolated case. Witness the more and more dangerous "greed scandals" that surfaced during the end days of the Reagan Administration. Graft and fraud were rampant and occurred mostly where the money was—in the Defense Department—where everyone that had business there was giving or taking money, it seemed. But, again, *this is not new in economic history.* Corruption always follows a period of currency debouchment, which brings inflation and greed grabbing, which develops a powerful hold on the mind of the consuming masses.

A HISTORY OF AMERICAN VIOLENCE

Since we read daily of crimes being committed, and of our prisons being filled, we somehow do not identify that built into most Americans is a string of inherent violence, as Commanger wrote:

> "The elementary fact which glares upon us from every chapter of our history and stares at us from every page of our daily paper is that the major, the overwhelming, manifestations of violence in our history and society have been, and still are, official. In America violence is clad in the vestments of respectability and armored with the authority of the law. It customarily took and takes the forms of assaults on the weak and the helpless, on the whole of society, on future generations. It is violence against the native peoples, Negroes, immigrants, women and children, perishing and dangerous classes. It is a

violence against nature herself."

Commanger continued:

"Violence takes many forms. Our daily speech testifies to the variety of meanings we read into the word. Thus we speak of violating territory; violating a treaty; violating a promise, an oath or law. Literature is filled with references to the violence of party faction; philosophy rebukes those whose notions violate logic or truth. When we speak of violating the rights of man that term has reference to more than the use of deliberate force: it embraces habitual misconduct by government or society."

CHAPTER TWO

REFERENCES

1. *Omni Magazine,* September 1989, Special Environmental Supplement.

2. Kapp, William K., *The Social Costs of Free Enterprise* (Schocken Books, NYC, 1971).

3. Bruce, H.R., *American Policies and Politics (The Making of American Democracy),* (Halt, Rinehart, Winston, N.Y. 1962).

CHAPTER THREE

MONEY—THE ROOT OF ALL EVIL?

One of the great lessons of economic history is that politicians have always been notoriously unreliable in their management of money. Back in history, the continual debasement of coined money had as much as anything to do with the origin of paper money in Europe. It was a form of protection against dishonest coinage.

Ironically, later on these newer forms of money managed by governments demonstrated their dishonesty on a far grander scale. China, great inventor of many things, invented paper money and began to circulate promises to pay which were printed on paper. The Chinese were centuries ahead of the West in recognizing the usefulness of this device in solving the perennial problem of all governments—how to raise money to pay their expenses. The Chinese stopped issuing paper in 1440, and did not do so again for over four hundred years, long after Western politicians discovered the device and began misusing it—as the Chinese had done a thousand years before.

The evolution of modern paper money started with mediaeval merchants trading over national boundaries, and with the rise of banders who have done so much damage in America. The real seed of modern money was the spreading realization that private individuals could be counted on to carry out their promises with regards to money. It is as old as time that politicians and other historical rulers could not be trusted.

Time after time, all through history, the public realized that it was not possible to know how much gold or silver would be contained in a given piece of currency. All that everyone knew with certainty was that it would be continually debased by clipping and sweating, that it would be counterfeited, and that the rulers themselves would be the counterfeiters issuing new coins with a lower metallic value made to masquerade, as closely as possible, the old coins. In some nations, annual re-coinages occurred, like our yearly models of automobiles, except that the coins year by year became poorer.

THE ETERNAL PROMISE OF GOOD TIMES

Why have rulers, all through the ages, wrecked money with astonishing regularity? Because the public has always demanded a period of economic good times. The only way to create good times is to create too much money. Of course, in our sophisticated time, long removed from metals, we have done this with computer-credit-money. We have created a long, false prosperity, a prosperity based on debt, not on the creation of real wealth, as it should have been. This last computer-credit-money experience in America and the world is the central culprit in destroying our economy and our social structure. And this brings us back to gold

WHY IS GOLD THE WORLD'S MONEY?

Gold is the only *real* money there ever was. It is the only money universally recognized and accepted, and governments cannot create either gold or silver—real money. The metals must be mined. Labor, and other forms of wealth than the metals themselves, are necessarily used up in obtaining them.

The government has to get possession of metals like everyone else. The government can do this in various ways: 1) By seizing it in the form of taxes or fines, 2) By selling privileges to its people like the right to incorporate, for example, 3) By exchanging the land it owns for gold, 4) By mining gold itself, and 5) By borrowing—issuing its promises to pay gold to those who have mined the gold or silver, or those who have otherwise acquired gold and silver.

The first and second reasons are normally the main ways that governments use to acquire the real money; that is, by taxes and the sale of privileges. The third, the sale of property, is only an occasional resource, as is the fourth—the mining of gold itself.

But the last means, borrowing from the public, is the most "modern" way to do this. And in America we have done this on an unparalleled scale—well over $12 trillion in borrowing and promises to pay has been created.

Governments cannot create real money, but like the rest of us must acquire it from its original owners. This is not true of credit money forms. This form of money the government and the private sector can create in great abundance. It should be obvious (but it is not) that the incredible notion that governments can create money is tied to the phoney identification of the promises inherent in credit money (borrowing) to pay money and money itself. And this is an important fact most frequently overlooked. It is a quicksand in which most get sunk.

What we believe is that the politicians, by designating the money of America (credit money), is registering the will of the people. This is not true. This action does not register the prevailing will, and these laws in a short time become dead-letter laws. Ruling elites all through history have attempted to control their citizens and have found themselves completely blocked by the power of the people. Nowhere is this more evident than in money—and we have Gresham's Law to prove it.

Sir Thomas Gresham was asked by the puzzled and worried Queen Elizabeth why it was that, as soon as she mined good gold or silver coins, they at once disappeared from circulation; only debased coins remained. He explained that poor money always drove good money out of circulation. But here is a paradox: Why doesn't the public demand newly minted gold and silver coins, and refuse to accept the debased coins? The truth is that the public knows what money is—a fixed weight of gold or silver of a certain quality. They prefer it so much that once they get their hands on it, they will only give it up when they can be sure to get full value in other goods. And when they get counterfeit money, they pass it on as fast as they can, knowing it to be worthless. Politicians can do nothing about this.

One example in American history was the attempt by the Continental Congress to make the ill-fated Continental Notes acceptable currency. Anybody who refused to accept them was legally to be regarded as an enemy and precluded from trade in the colonies. Another instance, shortly afterward, was the even more determined effort in revolutionary France to make their assignats acceptable in French commerce. Those who would not accept them in trade were subjected to a heavy fine, and this was later changed to the death penalty. In spite of these draconian measures, and of the additional fact that a handsome reward was offered for information as to breaking the law, the assignats continued to go their swift way to complete worthlessness and unacceptability.

The will of the people as to what real money shall be is supreme. The government's attempt to designate what the money will be for us in America (credit money) can only successfully exercise that power when it coincides with the will of the people. And until the depression, it functioned this way.

We now recognize this truth only when the debt-money we have used, because it has purchasing power, is destroyed in defaults, foreclosures, etc., leaving us penniless. Then we may learn that it was not real money at all. It was a promise. The promise has been broken. We must start anew.

IS AMERICAN MONEY DIFFERENT?

The debasing of money all through history is as old as time.

But there are generational gaps, and people forget that credit-money always reverts to debt, its original form. This development leads to poverty en masse. And it is this discovery that brings in its wake epic transformation of the society that brought this crisis through credit abuse.

In America we have wantonly destroyed the buying power of our credit money since it was advanced in the 1930s as a way to get the country out of depression. It was believed we could borrow our way to prosperity by the growing use of credit and money that carried interest to boot. It was an insidious process, and the dramatic decrease in purchasing power and credit money value was not noticed until the late 1970s when a burst in inflation emerged. This was the finalizing of a process that had been at work for forty years, and only then emerged as a Financial Titanic. But instead of destroying this credit during the liquidation process, the politicians took the opposite tack and increased the credit money still more. This gave us a temporary burst of good times and a deadly debt weight in the process.

With interest compounding, it led (as it had to) to borrowing to service the debt, pay the interest, with less and less being used to create wealth by bona fide purchasing.

Our society turned from wealth creation to debt creation with compound interest costs. There was no way this debasement of money could continue.

The extraordinary danger is that it has brought on the greatest Depression probably in all of recorded history. This abuse of money, on a global scale, was the culprit. It may bring deep seated change.

FUTURE TROUBLE FORESEEN

Former Secretary of State, Dean Acheson, addressed a Congressional Committee on Post War Economic Policy in November 1944. He said, "We cannot go through another ten years at the end of the Twenties and beginning of the Thirties without having the most far-reaching consequences upon our economic and social system." In 1950, President Truman said in a speech: "In 1932, the private enterprise system was close to collapse. There was real danger that the American people might turn to some other system. If we are to win the struggle between freedom and communism, we must be sure that we never let such a depression happen again."

Now it has.

CHAPTER FOUR

WHY INDUSTRIAL CAPITALISM SUCCEEDED

Most Americans have a deep faith in their economic system—industrial capitalism—and the consensus is that our system has been a winner since 1776 because: 1) Americans work harder, 2) Americans are more creative, 3) It is a natural American trait to be successful and a winner, so we applaud competition and winners, and 4) a wealth of other similar ideas.

In industrial capitalism, there were four things that could be sold:

1) Labor's use sells for wages.
2) Land's use sells for rent.
3) Goods sell for profit, as do services.
4) Use of money sells for interest.

A long-term view of industrial capitalism reveals another side of the success of our capitalistic society. From almost the beginning, the men who produced "goods" had a special advantage over those who got their income from land or from rent.

There was a dislocation of prices—a remarkable rise in the general price level due to the discovery of gold and silver in the New World—in the early days of capitalism (around 1500), which gave the price of goods a considerable advantage over the price of using land and the cost of labor. This meant that the merchant class, the producers, enjoyed a large advantage of relatively cheap rent and low wages while they sold their goods at steadily rising prices. As far back as 1549, it was known that rents lagged behind prices: "the most part of the landers of this Realm stand yet at the old Rent."[1] So, back in the beginning, it was not landowners or rent-takers as a class who became capitalists.

There is a lot of historical data on wages. In 1501, the index number of prices and wages in England stood at 95, with the period 1451-1500 as the base.[2] By 1700 the index had risen to 339, but the wage index stood at 233. This meant that while prices had risen 256%, wages had risen only 145%, and it was the same in France. During those two centuries actual wages had fallen with regard to prices, and laborers were in no way meant to be the capitalists of the new industrial society.

So, by simple elimination, we arrive at the door of those who benefited by the price upheaval: they were the men who had goods to sell. The landlords were losing, the workers were losing, but the entrepreneurs were gaining. Hamilton wrote: "For a period of almost two hundred years English and French capitalism—and those of other advanced countries—enjoyed incomes similar to the American producers from a similar spread between prices and wages from 1916 to 1919."[3]

Of the period from 1550 to 1650, John Maynard Keynes observed: "Never in the annals of the modern world has there existed so prolonged and so rich an opportunity for the business man, the speculator, and the profiteer. In these golden years, modern capitalism was born."[4]

But the producers also had something else going for them which made their lot an easy one: they got the windfall from the newly discovered raw materials from Columbus in 1492, and other voyagers. Hamilton continues: "The windfalls thus received, along with the gains from the East India trade, furnished the means to build up capital equipment, and the stupendous profits obtainable supplied an incentive for the fresh pursuit of capitalistic enterprise. During the seventeenth and late sixteenth centuries, England, France, and the Low Countries were seething with such genuinely capitalistic phenomena as systematic mechanical invention, company formation, and speculation in securities of financial and trading concerns. These developments were a significant step in the direction of the modern factory system, with the accompanying developments in commerce and finance."

So far, the low cost of things in general have been dealt with, but not the cost at the frontier, where they were found.

From 1500 to 1700 goods rode in the saddle, and it was the business of discovering them and bringing them to Europe that caused the growth of business activity in Europe since they were found in the New World and were then transported by sea, at the lowest cost, cheapening them additionally.

There were two kinds of windfalls: the frontier treasure of gold and silver, and the furs which were produced literally for free. Cheap labor skinned the animals, they were sent to Europe and sold at high prices, just like they are today. This was a primary windfall.

A secondary windfall came from the land: the plantation, the farm, the cattle business, etc. Remember, this was long ago and the land was free, despite any laws to the contrary. What wrecked early investors was not its first low cost, but the waiting period until it yielded its bounty. For example, the thirteen "plantations" established by England along the Atlantic coast illustrate what happened to investors: all the thirteen missed the quick return because they were north of the gold and south of the furs in a land where wealth waited on a lot of hard work to be done. By the time the work was done, the early investors were broke, and the people they had sent over were left to themselves.

The failure to find easy wealth or cheap labor resulted in suffering, famines, and death among the immigrants and financial loss to the English investors. It is a miracle that Virginia survived, but the survivors became the company and landholders and took their first step towards riches and freedom. And the growth of the tobacco industry proved it.

The cattle business in the west had so many free windfalls that it should be classed like gold, and it came at the end of the age of free land. The early cattleman had no investment or obligation to pay taxes and such. The feed was free, and he harvested his crop by having the cattle do all the work. And he also got hides as a byproduct. The automatic grazing of the cattle has to this day surpassed our best automation. It also eliminated labor as a significant cost, or a force to count.

So, the success of capitalism from the outset was based on discovery of free natural resources, and freedom to do what one wanted with them. This magical formula was a sure fire winner from the beginning: high prices, low costs, and bountiful profits.

And now comes the complicating factor and the one that has again changed our world forever: money and credit.

MONEY AND CREDIT

Keynes developed a theory of prosperity based on an idea of "profit inflation."[5] He also had a theory to deal with deflations and depression—the separate theory of "profit deflation." He believed the two combined determined the upswing and downswing of business cycles and the nation's welfare. The three factors Keynes believed to be paramount were: *profit, thrift, and enterprise.* He wrote, "It is enterprise which improves the world's possessions…. If Enterprise is afoot, wealth accumulates whatever may be happening to Thrift, and if Enterprise is asleep, Wealth decays whatever Thrift may be doing.

Thrift and enterprise were directly linked by a third factor, Profit, he continued, "For the engine which drives Enterprise is not Thrift, but Profit."

The lure of profit ignites business even up to now. Thrift, we still believe, furnishes the means by which the enterprise arrives at its destination: to claim a profit.

That theory, still alive today, held that the boom times come when capital accumulates to make a nation great, when enterprise is getting the lion's share of profits.

It is when investment is outrunning hoarding, when prices are outrunning costs, including wages.

Keynes asked, "Were the Seven Wonders of the World built by Thrift? I deem it doubtful." He meant, Do men build palaces out of their savings or do they build them only because they have made ventures in which they risked something and gained much?

Then Keynes dealt with the idea of "money" and its role in profit inflation. It is what suddenly liberated metals do to prices, and not the money itself, as wealth that turns the trick by raising prices above costs gives the chance for still more profits. Keynes in our modern period gave examples of profit inflation. He wrote, "It is the teaching of this Treatise that the wealth of nations is enriched...during profit inflation...at times...when prices are running away from costs."

But a broader view does *not* support Keynes' views since the booms were much larger and lasted longer than anything he dreamed of. Through all the bad and good times, and wealth came into the system from the exploitation of the frontier's resources and kept the system running superlatively. In sum, the frontier's free resources were always the primary source of the system's profits because, simply, goods are based on raw materials. If their prices are low, or free, then costs are bedrock and price markups of any kind provide ample profits.

But the U.S. economic system—and world systems, too— was running out of frontiers and free or cheap resources. The first free gain ended in the early 1970s when a long downwave in world economies commenced because resources were nearing exhaustion and costing more in the process.

It was the ending of "free" resources: land, oil, whatever.

But there was more to making a profit than that, important as it was. As Gardiner C. Means wrote in *Industrial Prices and Their Relative Inflexibility,* there are two different types of market operation: the traditional market in which supply and demand are equated by a flexible price, and the administered price in which production and demand are equated at an inflexible administered price (where economic adjustments are brought about by changes in volume of production while price changes are of secondary significance).[6] This was demonstrated in the middle of 1989 when the automobile companies refused to cut prices, but altered finance charges, and reduced production of cars when auto inventories became excessive. As the Depression wears on they were forced to cut prices and close factories, worsening the economic situation since they were so important to the goods sector of the U.S. economy, even in our recent past.

That inflexible price dilemma was also at the root of the present long decline in economic affairs. It was raw materials and price manipulation that gave the economic systems its continued life and expansion, and when that disappeared, the capitalistic system was doomed.

THE KEYNESIAN PARADOX

It was Keynes who, in the 1930s, proposed the idea of governments actively intervening in the economic system and borrowing, creating debt to commence good times and so keep the economy progressing.

Actually, the private sector has always dominated our form of economic system. The private sector's use of credit, debt, and its leverage, had been accelerating since before 1900 when America and the world began an epic transformation from economic societies dominated by industry and goods to societies dominated by finance and the pursuit of money...not goods, but money.

IS MONEY WEALTH?

No. But we have thought of money as wealth for all too long.

Wealth has always been the production of goods and services, and money its byproduct. But for many years we changed this historic truism and redefined it:

We believed that if it was true that making goods made money—a profit—that any avenue we might walk down that produced money would be just as rewarding and just as good for society.

Alas. Society benefits only when there is an abundance of goods and machines that employ the public, but the public adopted the view of the capitalists that money alone was enough...that money was wealth.

So, we started living in an upside down and inside out way. We worked for money, we revered it, and we became utterly dependant on it. All while this drive was in motion, we lost sight of the idea that the machines that made the goods that produced the work were needing fewer and fewer men and women, so the true source of wealth—production—was being done with less work and requiring less people. This was deadly in a society where the work ethic was of great importance.

So we had money wealth, less work, and the combination became lethal as everyone worked more to acquire money and without thought or regard for its only real source, goods making.

As pointed out in the next chapter, this shift of attention for one generation at least altered the base of capitalism from industrial production to finance capitalism.

But in the current crisis we realize the money wealth represented by paper has overnight become almost valueless, that it was all for naught. Many of us are now out of work, and there is no place for us to go now to find work.

The end result of this will be, if it has not already started, a time of disruption feeding through our entire society. Social unrest, political change, signs of the beginnings of a new culture, a reassessment of the past money-illusion and the way things were, and a time to change much of what presently seems familiar will occur.

And, as I note in a later chapter, we will probably spend a lot of time thinking about altering money as we have known it because of the damage it did to each and every one of us. We will probably abandon the concept of interest payments, and work with a form of money tomorrow that will be interest free.

Will this then reignite capitalism? Put a new dress on the old doll? No. It will be just another step of many we will make towards our society, and the way we go about making our living.

We are on the edge of epic change of all that seemed familiar, and this book may be a source book for you for coping and surviving the change now started.

There is resistance to change and new ideas because we don't like new "things." We want to hang on to yesterday, but we have gone too far with our old institutions and ways that have failed us. We all "know" that, but in our heart of hearts we do not want to admit yet that the old order and its ways are gone.

The new and unfamiliar are not friendly. Know that and understand why we must all prepare and change nonetheless.

LOOKING AT CHANGE

The idea of pursuing money alone for profit by ever increasing debts (which is what 95% of modern money is) was the main force that has led to our current savage breakdown.

We had come to believe that money by and of itself was the most important thing in our society and that goods and services production were secondary. Thus, the chase for money changed the idea from wealth creation of goods with money as its byproduct to money creation of still more money with goods and services following as its byproduct. Profit was money. Money was profit. The capital of building and equipment assumed a secondary role. Our lives, our destiny, and our minds changed from goods to money.

Since capitalistic societies were driven by the profit motive, whatever provided the most profit stole the show. As time progressed, it became apparent that the money men—the bankers, the usurers, etc.—were the ones creating the most profits in industrial capitalism, not the industrialists.

All through history, the money lender, and in our time the same man, has been in the forefront of the profit machine. It was his use and abuse of credit that brought us our business cycles, and as Fernand Braudel wrote in *Perspective of History,* the pursuit of money, for money's sake, has a long history to support the belief.[7] He noted, "From mid-13th Century to the start of the 16th Century, with Venice emerging as a world leader; from the 16th Century to the middle of the 18th Century, and ending of the first decade of the 19th century, led by London, and starting about 1900 and up the downturn in the early 1970s, New York leading. These were secular trends, shifting relations of dominance, major changes in the economic and political life." And they were all characterized by their focus of economic activity on acquiring money for money's sake.

CHAPTER FOUR

REFERENCES

1. *Hall's Discourse on the Common Wealth of This Realm of England,* 1545 (Harvard Univ. Press, 1934).

2. Hamilton, *American Treasure and the Rise of Capitalism (1500-1700),* Economica, No. V, 1926, p. 356.

3. Hamilton, *American Treasure and the Rise of Capitalism (1500-1700),* Economica, No. I, 1929, p. 316.

4. Keynes, John Maynard, *A Treatise on Money,* Vol. II (Harcourt, Brace & Co., N.Y.C., 1930), p. 156.

5. Keynes, John Maynard, *A Treatise on Money,* Vol. II (Harcourt, Brace & Co., N.Y.C., 1930), p. 148.

6. Means, Gardiner C., *Industrial Prices and Their Relative Inflexibility* (9. Doc. No. 1232, 74th Congress, 1st Session, 1, 8, 10-12, 27, 28).

7. Braudel, Fernand, *The Perspective of History* (Harper & Row, N.Y.C., 1984).

CHAPTER FIVE

INDUSTRIAL CAPITALISM (MAKING GOODS) AND FINANCIAL CAPITALISM (MAKING MONEY)

One of the riddles of the American economy has been the very long-term focus of attention and thought on the American economic system being primarily an industrial goods producing society—which it was before 1900. Capitalism was transformed from industrial capitalism to finance capitalism perhaps as early as 1900,[1] but policymakers and economic theorists were still stuck mentally in the industrial capitalism rut and slavishly followed every statistic that had to do with making goods.

For example, on April 4, 1989, the *Wall Street Journal* published an article on the release of statistical data by the National Association of Purchasing Management, who had surveyed new orders for goods, production, inventories, employment, and prices since 1931. According to the article, "Wall Street economists and traders generally regard the purchasing agents survey highly."

But this ancient and flawed analysis was even more deeply rooted. From the beginning of economic theory it has been believed that all wealth comes from the production of goods, and that credit was a by product. This was generally true all the way from 1500 to at least 1900. In the late 1800s America was furiously building its vast industrial base, but after the crises of

1893 and then of 1907, the economy quite unnoticeably was transformed from one driven by making goods to one driven by making money. The change was not visible, and it was later accelerated by the invention of the computer. This transformed money from paper and checks to blips on a screen traveling at the speed of light.

Finally it became apparent that the world of goods domination had become one of money domination. In capitalist economies, geared to profit making, it appeared suddenly that more profits could be gained from juggling money in its many and varied paper forms (mortgages, CD's, money market funds, etc.) than from making goods. For example, for many years the most profitable part of General Motors Corporation was its credit-extending arm, General Motors Acceptance Corporation (GMAC). And this was true of the burgeoning Japanese economy, too, as Nissan made more from "juggling money" in 1988 than they did from making automobiles.

As an example of this global change, by 1986 world trade was made up of $2 trillion of goods transfers, and $36 trillion of capital transfers.[2] This ratio fit equally as well within each national boundary: in America we not only made more cars than could be sold, but we made more money and still more money from making money. According to former Federal Reserve Chairman Paul Volcker before a Congressional Committee on April 26, 1986, the ratio of debt to income (Gross National Product) which had been constant for years at 140%, increased in the 1980s to 170%, and finally rose to 200%. The meaning of this shift was that more activity was taking place in money-making activities than in goods-making activities.

EARLY BANKING

Going back to the beginning of the Industrial Revolution, it was believed that making goods produced wealth, so every effort should be made to produce goods. From the beginning, getting funds to make goods was a problem. So banking systems were developed to create credits necessary to meet the demand of industry for capital equipment—savings were gathered and directed to industry: industrial loans. One of the central ideas of economic theory was that increasing capital goods-making would increase total wealth. Thus, the production of goods always had all the funds it required and this gave us, finally, a surplus of productive capacity in the making of goods. But, alas, in this process, there was no money similarly created for the distribution and consumption processes.

This created an enormous problem throughout U.S. economic history, since technology increased productive capacities far beyond the distribution system's capacity to absorb them. It never became apparent to the authorities that it was the distribution mechanism that should have been overhauled or scrapped, and especially the distribution-money-system. The result, all through time, was the great over-production of capital even though much of it was idle. This crucial flaw had to be centered in the money system: producers depositing collateral and paying interest could always have money created for them by banks to enable them to produce at the expense of the whole community. But in this very same system there was no money created for distribution. No one thought of how to similarly supply money to consumers to help them consume as it had been to producers to enable them to produce.

But, there was an even deeper problem—that was the fact that, as time went on, fewer and fewer workers were able to produce more and more goods, so the traditional method of paying by wages broke down. This led to the vast extension of credit to consumers by producers and banks and a wide variety of other financial institutions that were invented to fill this income gap, heralding the change to finance capitalism.

Because of high rates of interest which compound seemingly without end, the consumer never really "owned" his material acquisitions—he "owed" them. This vast difference led all too often to financial breakdowns—manias, panics, and crashes—and American history has been dotted with fallout ever since 1800. Actually, however, credit abuse has a long history of precipitating crises—since 1300, at least.

But in a traditional system the benefits should not be conferred on just the producer-group to the exclusion of others—the difference between the acquisition of wealth and the creation of it (by whomever). This monkeying with the quantity of money by pretending to lend it and creating it, by pretending to repay it and destroying it, resulted only in some acquiring more at the expense of others. The supposed advantage it originally had of stimulating production as distinct from consumption became a disadvantage. But, more than that, evil has come from the standpoint of the whole nation. The variable money unit which gave short weight to one set of people and overweighting to another was not only unfair but a system-wrecker.

In our time, the problem became very much worse since the automation and computerization of production required fewer workers to produce ever larger quantities of goods, and the purchasing power distributed by industry, as wages, became increasingly insufficient to distribute their products—i.e., sell them.

This process, a long time ago, gave birth to producers lending to consumers. It was started in the U.S. in the 1920s, and "installment credit" was born. Back then the lenders ran into a hostile generation of savers and thrifty Americans, a carryover from the early days of the U.S. industrial challenge. But the spread in lending to the public continued and, after the World War II savings were consumed by the public in an orgy of spending, it became necessary to lend more and more to the public so they could buy the bounty industry easily produced.

By the late 1980s, the public owed on installment credit alone over $700 billion at very high rates of interest. The switch from industrial capitalism to finance capitalism was large, but no one was looking—we were busy counting automobile inventories.

COMPOUND INTEREST

Bankers and other large corporate lenders have demanded interest from the beginning of time, but at much higher rates in our time. Although reviled by the Bible, interest has survived to our time where it has become a given. Still, the laws of compound interest have been ignored by the borrowers. Simple interest, where interest is periodically paid, became publicly known when the public sought high rates of return during the brief inflationary period in America—when rates rose sharply in the late 1970s. But compound interest, which is not periodically paid (by definition), kept on invisibly taking its toll on the American economic system. Compound interest was properly called "that which plows on Sunday." By 1988 this sum was over $1 trillion per year, a form of tribute paid on $11 trillion in domestic debt to those who loaned the funds. This represented a vast transfer of wealth from wages to capital. Something was wrong.

During the late 1970s a few people began to question the soundness and sensibility of paying interest. Why, some thought for example, would the federal government pay interest to borrow money for public purposes? This seemed absurd. The government should, at least in theory, be able to borrow on its own creditworthiness and pay no interest. But this did not happen. President Lincoln, among others, railed at this injustice. But the system continued on unchanged.

This payment of interest may have been the fatal flaw in our capitalistic economic system. Real output in America only grew in years in which the aggregate demand grew; demand grew only when the money supply grew; the money supply grew only when debt grew. The longer output, demand, the money supply and debt grow, the higher the rate of interest becomes and the more excessive the growth of interest and debt.

HOW WE GOT ON THIS TREADMILL

The Industrial Revolution and its newly formed democratic

governments gave birth to the individual as an important persona, and, in the process, lifted the burden of human labor and made effort more productive. It took the harness off the human horse and put it on inanimate horsepower. It was the emergence of the individual that gave American society its dynamic quality, its flashing vitality, its amazing energy. This change brought the stimulus Americans always had and which appeared as a seemingly unending inborn desire to acquire more material things. This overwhelming trait made Americans focus more on money and acquiring it than on any other one thing.

By the 1980s, everyone in America worked and talked and thought about nothing but money and how to acquire more of it. And, of course, this craving fed the credit-money-machine—the borrowing and lending at interest to the flash point where the society became too burdened with debt and simply broke down under its dead weight.

A "JUGGLING MONEY" ECONOMIC SYSTEM

Industrial capitalism—the industrial society—has been changed since the last Great Depression. We now have a society that grows and functions by "juggling money." This has created a new social order in which those who manage and make money make more profits and have more power than those who manage, make and move goods. The latter group were the auto makers, chemical makers, steel producers, etc. The former group includes bankers, financial services industry people, merger-makers, and credit jugglers.

But in a society driven by profit, men and women seek the work that makes the most money, and this has evolved into the making money businesses. Truly, the money that money makes, makes money. And this is now true in another form, called juggling money, as distinct from compound interest where that phrasing was derived. Now it is business activity devoted to juggling credit dollar money.

Back in the 14th century this also happened, and it was learned then that money made by work was more lasting and more beneficial to society than money made with money. One promoted thrift and growth, the other greed and speculation.

In our time, Paul Volcker, former Chairman of the Federal Reserve, said in a speech on May 14, 1987, "As nation, as businesses, as individuals we are spending more than we produce. We can only do that by borrowing heavily.... We are busy mortgaging our future.... In the process we are risking financial turbulence...we are in danger of losing control of our economic destiny."

The private financial sector, as I wrote in *How to Profit From the Next Great Depression,* has silently created its own vast credit creating machine, outside of any control by the Federal Reserve System or the U.S. Treasury and they furiously drove down their own way creating credits on a colossal scale and profiting from this endeavor all along the road.

Thus enormous transfer of power—since money is power in America—was not "seen." Instead, we were all focusing on how many houses and cars were made—the manufacturing sector—because our economic theories told us that that was the center of economic activity and wealth-making. But it was not. It had been changed.

In the 1980s, credits were created by huge lending by a diverse group of financial institutions: General Motors Acceptance Corporation, for example, issued $89 billion in auto loans. Equitable Life Insurance Company—and other insurance companies who are sometimes called "the invisible bankers"—also created credits because of the vast resources they controlled. They loaned for home construction, office buildings, and bought vast amounts of securities offered privately as well as through the traditional stock exchange system. Investment Bankers on Wall Street (Drexel Burnham, Kohlberg, Kravis, Roberts, for example) created over $200 billion of what were called "junk bonds," throwing more credits into the U.S. credit money supply system. The Bank of Japan, the Taiwan Stock Exchange, the Hong Kong Banking system, all fed credits into our financial system, creating them globally. The U.S. Banks created trillions of credits on their own—credit cards, loans of all sorts without regard to waiting for the traditional textbook Federal Reserve controls of adding more banking reserves. Instead, they could (and did) borrow funds domestically and globally building a gigantic pool of credit money outside federal control.

BANKERS IN THE SADDLE

This rise to power of money men was chronicled in the *Economist* magazine in a description of the rise to power of the Morgan Stanley New York investment bank.[3] This firm, on its own, started investing its own capital in leveraged buy outs as far back as 1985, and made a total of 40 investments amounting to $230 million. By 1989 the market value of this investment had risen four times to over $900 million, realizing huge capital gains. Then they made still more money from sales of merchant-bank investments. Their returns year after year averaged over 20% on their investments, doubling their funds every five years.

In 1989 there was a large financial organization in Dallas, Texas, called Associates Corporation. It was purchased by Ford Motor Company on July 28, 1989, who made a statement that they expected this firm to provide them in the future with over 30% of their net income. Ford bought this company from the movie maker Paramount, who had derived 49% of their income from juggling money instead of from making movies.

Thus the power and business activity shifting to the money game—paper credits shuffling back and forth in the trillions of dollars each year. They were so vast that they had to be transferred electronically by the Federal Reserve electronic wire transfer system (sending credit dollars by computers), and also by the clearing system of the New York Clearing House who, in the old days, cleared checks by hand; now the total transfers by both institutions were over $1 trillion per day by computers.

During this period the names of the money men in the public eye were Milken, Boesky, Volcker—not Ford or Chrysler. The names changed and so did the fundamental economic activity.

But all of this activity had as its foundation credit and debt. And the lesson of history is that debts are always paid. Either you pay or you default. Beyond that, the more credit issued the less the quality inherent in the loans. So, the system ran out of qualified borrowers, or those who had the resources or could earn them to repay the loans they had acquired diminished in size.

So, the end result of this process is that the vast credit expansion since 1945 would turn into its reverse—credit contraction—and the development of this process would bring ruin to us all.

This is what has happened and this is where we are in 1990.

WHY THIS DEPRESSION WILL BE SO SAVAGE

All of the American depressions since 1800—and there were five between 1800 and 1900—were rooted in the collapse of the manufacturing sector which caused huge employment and had a ripple effect throughout the economic system. This led to economic theories which called for creating demand by government borrowing and feeding through to consumers to spend and buy goods so this artificial stimulus would get industry back on track, hiring people and renewing the economic good times.

Now it is different. The vast expansion of credit dollars, and the burgeoning financial services industry of brokers, analysts, insurance men/women, salesmen without end, and much of it magnified by using margin or leverage (meaning a small down payment and the rest being borrowed funds), has led us into the most dramatic and catastrophic financial collapse in world history. And, it is also on a global scale.

So, where will the credits come from to restore our society? To carry us through the hard times? To get America going again?

Where?

THE SHIFT OF WEALTH

Over long-term spans the original wealth found in the New World went through several major distributions. In the beginning, it was taken over by monarchies, given to them literally by explorers sent out to find the booty. This period lasted from about 1500 to 1700.

But starting about 1600 and lasting to 1900, this same wealth was moving from the sovereigns to the people. In America this took the form of credit expansions which grew steadily larger over time.

And from 1900 to 1990 the wealth was again moving, but now from the people to the government—through the credit system—as the federal government became the final and ultimate creditor. But in this final and epic shift of the weight of debt, interest compounding like topsy, and its quality diminishing rapidly, may lead to national bankruptcy.

There is no bank of last resort—the bank is broke. The ultimate guarantor, Uncle Sam himself, can become "not creditworthy."

National bankruptcies are as old as economic history, but the experience will be brand new to Americans. So, the question arises, how will we survive? How will we make it?

We will. That is the good news message of this book.

DEBT MATURITIES

One of the oldest measures of creditworthiness of anyone, whether it is an individual, corporation or government, is the length of time that each one can borrow for. Is it safe to lend your funds to a government for long periods? In England a long time ago the credit of the government was perceived to be so strong that they issued, and the public bought, securities that had no maturity—they were issued for perpetuity.

But that has all changed because the government has borrowed too much.

Like any other debtor, the more debt the government issues, the less creditworthy it is. So, over time, the average maturity of federal government debt has steadily declined. Now all of its debt matures on an average of four and one-half years. This means the government must go into the financial markets every year for no less than $800 billion to roll over maturing debt and borrow the little new debt they need.

The more they borrow, the less time they can get from lenders. This is another historic danger signal of great importance and its significance can be seen in the debt travails of Brazil during 1989.

Brazil borrowed too much money at interest rates that were so high that it made it impossible for the debts to be repaid, regardless of what they did to their internal economy to try and accomplish this. The result of this steady decline in their creditworthiness as a nation brought them to the financial brink when in was revealed that their total domestic debt maturity had shrunk to one day![4] They were compelled to borrow $50 billion dollars a day to keep the country running. Obviously, they could not manage this debacle forever, and perhaps by this time they will have defaulted on all of their foreign debts. This event will whip the monetary world into a financial frenzy. And if not by now, then it is still coming.

So, the lesson of history is clear for America, and the growing short debt maturities is another harbinger of ill winds that are blowing across America.

THE EPIC TRANSFORMATION

Thus, the stage is now set for another epic transformation. A new, revitalized money system is bound to emerge from the ruins of our recent past credit abuses, probably one totally transformed into debt-free money.

There will also be another shift of money: from the defunct government back to the people. This massive shift will destroy in its wake giant corporations, and lead to a new age of small business, the entrepreneur, something more akin to the original idea of capitalism, about which so much has been written.

FUNDAMENTAL CHANGE

It is remarkable that all through history the really fundamental changes in societies have come about not from the dictates of governments, or results of battles, but through vast numbers of people changing their minds—sometimes just a little bit.

Now, as we wee these disruptions in our lives, we will—all of us—change our minds about the way we have lived and react by welcoming the change. A new order is then in the making—an upheaval.

THE AGE OF POLITICS IS ENDING

The Age of Religion ended several hundred years ago. It was replaced by the Age of Politics, a by-product of the industrial society. But now that Age, too, is ending along with capitalism.

During the Age of Politics, the most basic delusion was that of popular participation, control and problem-solving.

Perhaps one of the great evils, from which the other evils sprang, was the politization—the act of suffusing everything with politics, and dragging it into the political arena—down to the last vote at a PTA meeting, for example. In our world in America, contrary to what was the rule in all previous ages throughout history, everything is politicized. We seek political solutions for everything under the sun, whether the problem is freedom, justice, peace, prosperity, happiness, whatever—we want someone else to take care of the problem for us.

Because of this politization of all aspects of life and the orienting of all our thought towards politics, men have increasingly turned to the State for the solution of their problems. But, the State could not solve them even if it tried.

This growing tendency to turn to the State has led to three great evils: 1) Boundless growth in the State's size and power; 2) growing dependance on it by the individual; 3) a continuing decrease in the control over it by the public who believe they control it. What they have really done is surrender their own powers to the politicians.

The State then engaged in politics. And even though the State ceaselessly talks through the mass media—through those who represent it, whether they are democratically elected or not—of noble things and cherished values, momentous decisions and great goals, essentially the State deals with tinder. Two things always limit all political endeavors: 1) Politics itself follows set patterns over which politicians have absolutely no control; 2) where a certain margin of freedom of actions remains, they deal with the marginal, the ephemeral, the basically unimportant things that are made to seem important by them for public consumption. The politicians merely manipulate the images among which the public deals.

Back in the Middle Ages, man had direct knowledge of the limited range of things that concerned him. But now man lives in a world of images reflecting faraway places, people and conditions brought to him as "information" by the powerful mass media. The information is not a tissue of lies, but it permits many interpretations and translations. And, the worse the real news is, the more "managed" and "edited" will be the version fed to the public. Then the whole of these spurious images is translated by the public into their view of the world. Alas.

Is the "public," then, without any influence upon the course of political events? Quite the contrary, their influence is all for the worse. This is because if public opinion is not aroused, nothing can be done in a democracy. But, if it is aroused, moderate, fair, and provident solutions are no longer possible. Public opinion has a habit of either disregarding something altogether or demanding a drastic—an unjust and undesirable—

solution.

There are three main aspects of this delusion: The first concerns over who controls the State. In the real world in a democracy, as we practiced it in America, the public does not control it as they think they do. The public does control who is on top of the pyramid, but that does not at all mean they control the State. The elected representatives also do not control the State.

If you try to change those in office, it really means nothing since they deal almost entirely with ephemeral matters or "playing the political game." Because of this, they are not effective leaders. lastly, in our past high-tech age, they are servants of the technical experts they hire to guide them.

The second aspect of the political delusion is that of popular participation. If the public cannot control the State, do they not at least participate much in what it does? No. Just as their votes cannot control the course of events, their political parties/associations and so on do not channel popular desires in order to make them effective. Beyond that, members of the rank and file, like the citizens of the State, depend on the information fed them, and those in command—public leaders—are experts in managing information and in preventing nonconforming forces and ideas from emerging.

Lastly, there is the eternal wish and grasp for "political solutions." After peace, freedom, education, the living standard, etc., has been advertised and accepted as a political problem, then people demand still more political solutions to all sorts of other problems. But there are no political solutions for these problems—we cannot politicize our educational system and make it better, for example. In fact, in the real world there are no political solutions for even genuine political problems. Just because arithmetic problems have solutions does not mean political problems can have them. Despite this, the bureaucrats/technocrats more and more present to us political problems as solvable equations. Because we believe politicians, we expect politics to find solutions.

CHAPTER FIVE

REFERENCES

1. Adams, Brooks, *The Law of Civilization & Decay* (Alfred A. Knopf, 1912).

2. *Harper's Magazine,* Index, March 1986, p. 7.

3. *Economist Magazine,* September 30, 1989.

4. *World Link,* September-October 1989.

CHAPTER SIX

SIGNS OF ECONOMIC CRISIS

By early 1990 there was a growing awareness at many levels in America that the Age of Debt was ending, that it would be replaced, as it always had been historically, by a newly-found conservatism in money matters—that the borrow and spend mentality born in the 1930s had finally shot itself in its foot.

During the early 1990s an old historical paradox again emerged: growing visible prosperity with invisible rot. The gross national product grew, but creditworthiness, in all sectors which financed it, fell. There were increases in personal income in nominal terms, but not real terms, with an increase in personal bankruptcies. Bank failures, corporate bankruptcies and falling profits were accompanied by rising stock prices. We had the appearance of good times with the reality of a dangerous basic economic disease starting to emerge.

The American standard of living was falling. The average worker's real income had been falling since 1973, but his debts had been rising all during that time period to the point where 70% of his income in 1990 was consumed by mortgage and installment debts.

Why had the nation's productivity steadily declined? Why are our debts so enormous, and why do we still have 3 million plus people out of work? How is it possible that the United States had been reduced to offering as its principal exports the bulk of cargos of scrap and waste paper? Who made off with the spirit of American enterprise?

Why have our large corporations been reduced to seeking financial and other aid from Washington ranging from savings and loan bailouts, to cut-rate timber leases, to toxic cleanups, and leaving the taxpayer to foot the bill? A gross example of corporate welfare was the millions of dollars in Urban Development Action Grants and other subsidies given to General Motors to build an automated Cadillac plant in Detroit. There were many other examples of these grants going to profitable companies along with a large menu of other direct grant and subsidy programs. There were even subsidies for exporting nuclear power plants and tobacco. The overall value of these corporate welfare payments amounted to more than $100 billion a year.

Going back to the 1970s, there was the $250 million Lockheed loan guarantee, and the $1.5 billion Chrysler loan guarantee, which by 1990 looked like small change. The taxpayer bailout of the savings and loan industry could well run well above $300 billion. Estimates of cleanup costs for U.S. nuclear weapon plants, managed by private firms such as DuPont and North American Rockwell, ran from $50 billion to $150 billion.[1]

There are other examples of decline and decay, but they failed to catch the attention of the average American who continued to dwell on America's past. Why did the illusions and delusions continue? Adolph A. Berle, Jr., a friend of capitalism but under none of its illusions, wrote in *Power Without Property,* "We live under a system of capitalism described in obsolete terms. We have come to believe our own repeated declarations that our society is based on individual initiative—whereas, in fact, most of it is no more individual than an infantry division. We assume our economic system is based on 'private property,' yet most of the industrial property is no more private than a seat in a subway train, and indeed it is questionable whether much of it can be called 'property' at all. We indignantly deny that we are collectivist, yet it is demonstrable that more than two-thirds of our enterprise is that the State did not do the collectivizing. We think of capital as the fruit of individual savings, whereas it really is the result of various methods of compulsion. Further, all capital is not alike."[2]

The American spirit of optimism goes far back in U.S. history. For example, before the stock market crash of 1929, John J. Raskob, formerly a top executive of General Motors and at the time Chairman of the Democratic National Committee, told his fellow Americans how all of them could and should become wealthy:

> "If a man saves $15 a week and invests in good common stocks, and allows the dividends and rights to accumulate, at the end of twenty years he will have at least $80,000, and an income from investments of around $400 per month. He will be rich and because income can do that, I am firm in my belief that anyone can not only be rich, but ought to be rich." [3]

So our belief system has deep roots.

Jean Gimpel, a scholar of medieval history, dispelled the notion of perpetual prosperity in *The Medieval Machine*.[4] The major reasons we believe that "we are the first" was found in the character of our high school history lessons. (Events and people were traditional and superficial. Deeper events were selectively taught. Few historians have studied the history of technology, Gimpel wrote, because they preferred to show man as a worker— working with his hands, making the world move, etc.)

After the energy crisis in the mid-1970s, a fear arose that Western technological society could be doomed to decline seriously and perish like all the world's previous civilizations. Gimpel asked, "Will our machine technics, our railways, cars, ships and airplanes disappear like the Roman roads and the Wall of China? Even our skyscrapers in ruins as in Babylon?"

The Middle Ages, Gimpel discovered, was one of the great

inventive eras of mankind. Between the tenth and thirteenth centuries, three hundred years, Western Europe experienced a technological boom. Both the boom and subsequent decline offer striking parallels to Western industrial society since 1950, the pre-crash situation in the United States. Some features of this first Industrial Revolution seem strangely familiar:

1) Great increase in population; new lands were colonized, new towns built.

2) Conditions favored free enterprise, leading to the rise of the self-made man.

3) Capitalist companies were formed and their shares sold.

4) Ruthless business methods were introduced to stifle competition.

5) There was an extensive division of labor and strikes by workers.

6) Energy consumption increased strikingly.

7) The use of machines was greatly expanded; tasks formerly done by hand were done by machines.

8) The general standard of living rose.

9) The growth of industry led to extensive pollution, posing a threat to the environment with long-term consequences.

10) Entrepreneurs extracted large profits and developed accounting and banking techniques.

11) The period was characterized by a spirit of optimism, a rationalist attitude and a firm belief in progress.

This sounds very familiar. But at a certain point, the dynamics of the Middle Ages began to fail, and symptoms of decline became evident—as ours are now.

1) The population ceased to grow.
2) Differences between classes hardened, and there was less social mobility.
3) Restrictive practices were introduced in many industries.
4) Unrest grew in large industrial centers.
5) The level of efficiency was dropping while at the same time there was greater resistance to change.
6) Energy production had peaked, and the standard of living began to decline.
7) Inflation began to get out of hand, currencies were devalued and banks crashed.
8) Established moral values declined. People became less public spirited and more permissive.
9) Man turned from traditional religion to embrace new esoteric cults.

The decline back then turned into a major colossal depression that lasted for one hundred years.

As Oswald Spenger wrote years ago, "The history of this technics is fast drawing to an inevitable close. It will be eaten from within like the grand forms of any and every culture."

Why can't we be different? Why must we repeat the same mistakes as other nations have in running their system?

The answer to that is to be found in the constancy of human behavior. People rarely change, and the change when that does happen is spread over many years and moves with glacial speed. We will, therefore, act like others have done all though history before us:

1) We will be stunned with the hard times we are now in.
2) We will see our greed vanish overnight and be replaced with a terrible fear. Nothing concentrates a man's mind as the loss of income and being unable to even buy bread, for example.

3) Social unrest will emerge on a huge sale, a form of modern barbarianism. This was prophesied in 1857! In a letter addressed to H.S. Randall, Esq., dated London, May 23, 1857, Lord MaCauley made the following prediction regarding America's future troubles: "Your Republic will be pillaged and ravaged in the twentieth century just as the Roman Empire was by barbarians of the fifth century, with this difference, that the devastation of the Roman Empire came from abroad, while your barbarism will be the people of your own country, and the product of your own institutions." [5]

Where are our barbarians in America today? 1)The minority groups in our society who have been largely left out of the mainstream, 2) with over two million homeless who, all to often, represent patients released from mental institutions as a by-product of calmative drugs developed during the 1970s, and 3) many others who believe they have, for whatever reasons, simply been "left out."

DECLINE OF THE WASP

There have developed over the years broken connections in the American social structure. Fifty years ago there was a clear American moral and civic identity. It was Anglo-Saxon in cultural inheritance. Protestant and Puritan in religion (white anglo-saxon-protestant—WASP). The elite that controlled the country's banking and industry and nominated its government were from a limited number of universities, originally Protestant, still secular instructors of a Protestant ethic. Immigrants, blacks, Jews and Asians—all who did not belong to this majority were made powerfully aware of their effect and submitted to intense pressures to conform and assimilate. It was a parochial America, an intensely limited one, but connected.

This America was destroyed somewhere between the start of World War II and the end of the Vietnam War. The vast population displacement of the war, the mass move West and South, the migration of blacks from farms to big cities, non-European immigration, affluence, television, the decline of the churches, the successful self-assertion of minorities, the elite leadership's humiliation in the Vietnam War, and want ensued, all combined to undo that America.

Americans of fifty or older know how profound change has been produced. No doubt much good was done for many. Out of this, however, has come an America of morally isolated people, no longer connected to a culture deeper or more responsible than that provided by the mass entertainment industry, a people for too many of whom "fun" is what life is all about, if it is about anything.

There is a moral void in America and it is where too many people in the United States existed in 1990. This insures vast change...a nation of discontents is a dangerous place.

"Security"—personal and financial—is highly valued by most Americans, though it is largely ignored and taken for granted. In the late 1980s, however, many areas in major cities became war-zones and poor residents were prisoners in their own homes because of root change in our culture and the breakdown in secure systems. So, when social disorder starts now warlords may emerge in control of cities and lawlessness will be the order of the day.

We are a population now undergoing dramatic and drastic change, and such a population is a population of misfits, and misfits live and breathe in an atmosphere of passion. There is a close connection between lack of confidence and the passionate state of mind, and the passionate intensity all around us now will be serving as a substitute for confidence most people have lost.

As this condition grows in America in 1990 and 1991, the stage will be set for a major political changes.

So, the "soft decline" so widely observed and heralded in the

1980s will not be an easily solvable problem. It will, instead, feed on itself as it grows and accelerates into a social, cultural, and political breakdown of our institutions and changes in our social structure.

To turn things around, to get America going again, will not be easy because to turn the population into effective men of action, there must be an abundance of opportunities and a tradition of self-reliance. This is quite the opposite of the world we have just left. If we had not lost those traits before these hard times, we would see an orgy of action by the public.

But missing those vital ingredients we will see a population faced with meager opportunities for action and one that will seek substitutes for the past political, social, and cultural systems.

It is the drastic change we are now living in that sets the stage for some kind of revolution. The revolutionary mood and temper are generated by the irritations, difficulties, hungers, and frustrations inherent in this realization of drastic change.

Since the depression we are now in will be a long one, the populace will not long tolerate its stunning impact on their lives, and will demand and get change. That cannot be avoided.

The hard times we are in has closed the doors to opportunity for most Americans, and this loss of self-confidence and self-esteem must lead to disastrous results. Europe at the turn of the fifteenth century—when the frontier booty was first discovered—saw a similar release of the individual from the corporate pattern of an all-embracing Church. At the outset, the release was accidental. The weakened and discredited church lost its hold on the minds and souls of the people of Europe. The emerging European individual at the end of the Middle Ages faced a breathtaking vista of new continents just discovered, new trade routes just opened, the prospect of fabulous empires yet to be stumbled upon, and new knowledge unlocked by the introduction of paper and printing. The air was charged with great expectations and there was a feeling abroad that by the exercise of his capacities and talents, and with the aid of good fortune, the individual on his own was equal to any undertaking at home and across the sea.

That fortuitous combination of circumstances, that fateful change from a communal to an individual existence, produced an outburst of vitality that has been the characteristic of America and marks it off from any other civilization. But that transformation was not smooth with the convulsions of the Reformation and Counter-Reformation which stemmed from the fears and passionate intensities of people unequal to the burdens and strains of individual existence.

Now we are coming full circle: again we leave the corporate existence and are thrown on our own as individuals. But this time there is no frontier to exploit. We are individuals living amidst the debris of the decayed system we were bred and raised in. We see chaos around us and little opportunity.

Will we try to reformulate the past, breathe new life into that dead horse? No. We will get our lives going again in a dramatically changed system.

IS IT THE END OF THE AMERICAN ERA?

The American Era could be ending. Why must this be? Can't we just go through another long Depression, like in the 1930s, and start up again? No. This time it could be different, because of some root transformations:

1) We can face future social unrest on a national scale with no parallel in our past. The public is obviously perceiving the entire system differently than it ever did before. They are upset, angry, and want and demand change, the signals of social change that emerged with the generation of 1968 were noticed by the public briefly. However, they were deep rooted and made a dramatic change in the way many of the younger generation perceived our affairs, the way they looked at our society. They did not like what

they saw: cities falling into ruin, homeless people everywhere, drugs, soaring crime rates, an increasingly unstable money system, and so on—all signs of change impending.

2) A nation that built its foundation and growth on credit was fine as long as wealth was created that repaid the growing credit use. But now we have a nation sinking—insolvent at every level—under a debt load created by our national abuse of credit. We have not produced; we have consumed. We must pay for this folly with episodic change.

3) As I have explained, in 1776, when America became America, there was a vast territory to exploit and develop. The resources were there for the taking, and Americans did just that. There is nothing wrong in any way with that process but, like all good things, the resources finally ran out. Now the process has reversed: the costs of replacing the exhausted natural resources have soared. In the wake of extraordinary economic growth we were left with foul air, foul water, and an environment that was rapidly becoming a disaster. No solutions emerged with things as they were. Change was being made. But there was a large inertia in the system, so, as other societies have done, patchwork solutions emerged—a short-run focus— but no basic changes by the ruling Old Guard were to be found.

A LOOK BACK

As the Industrial Revolution progressed, starting around 1500 and up until now, so did the concentration of people in cities. By 1988 the Census Bureau estimated that 75 percent of all Americans lived in what they defined as "metropolitan areas"—cities and towns of over 50,000 people.

Gone forever were the days when people could go, in different times, back to the farm for food, or to the small town for friendship and private welfare. The New Deal saw this private welfare system break down and transformed it into government relief for corporations and banks and people. But the New Deal was able to do this back then because America was a rich country with a high credit rating, virtually free of debt, so running deficits was easy. To aid the society with debt was believed to be not only good but right. The idea that debt was beneficent came ingrained in all of our systems and our souls. It became a way of life.

Although the process of debt has been reviled since Biblical times, it was, in our time, transformed into a power that would bring us prosperity. Why did we change from equity and saving to debt and not saving?

One of the main reasons for the extraordinary growth in public debt was that the historical and traditional stigma attached to fiscal deficits and debt growth gave way to a nonchalance on the part of politicians. For awhile large debts did not need to be justified, did not have political repercussions, and many economists and politicians came to see them as virtuous.

This growth was due to the high expectations of the role that governments should play with respect to income maintenance, job creation, and income distribution. Government intervention was pushed forward continually. The Federal Government then began to subsidize public services and made them cheap to users, and so raised the demand for them. And the public came to believe that it was their natural right to cheap and free health care, transportation, communications, etc. The spread between the private cost of using these services and the social costs of providing them introduced enormous and growing burdens on the Federal budgets. If the cost of those services had been totally covered by ordinary revenues, we would have seen a process of income distribution in favor of lower-income users of these services and be without fiscal deficits. But while the public wanted higher spending, they also wanted to pay less taxes.

Doesn't the cry for lower taxes ring a familiar bell? After all, for over a generation, every politician worth his salt recommended lower taxes as a key to more growth and prosperity. And in any referendum, no matter how trivial, the public can be counted on to vote against taxes.

The old idea that you should not borrow unless the investment would produce income to repay the borrowed money was abandoned in favor of government debt creation that made full employment and welfare the main objectives of economic policy. Then a whole generation of economists developed theories to rationalize this phenomena.

This change in the way we look at and think about debt has brought us the very hard economic times we are now in. Americans started becoming addicted to credit in the late 1920s.

As Dicton Wecter wrote, in *The Age of the Great Depression,* "Intensive campaigns were taken to break down 'sales resistance'—often insufficient purchasing power among small citizens—which led to new extensions of the time-payment plan for cars, clothes, electric washers, furniture, and jewelry. In effect, the latter lacked cash and the former, with his urgent need for sales, preferred this method to that of increasing mass purchasing power by cutting prices and boosting wages."[6]

Back in the 1930s, the Great Depression brought to light that such an economic system with inflated prices and exorbitant carrying charges would suffer great pain.

But in our time the debts have been larger and more pervasive. Our entire society is laboring under unrepayable debts with extraordinary interest costs, and there is no federal government to turn to for help now as there was during the first Great Depression. Back then, Uncle Sam was liquid. It easily borrowed and funded people, banks, and corporations, and got America running again.

Now we are at the pole: the entire system is bankrupt, insolvent. Where will we get the resources to finance tomorrow?

THE RAINY DAY IS HERE

It has been estimated that by 1988 more than 2 million potholes are filled each year in New York City. With current funding, that city could complete replacement of their obsolete sewer system in 300 years. In New Orleans in 1988, they were still using sewage equipment that they installed in 1896, having bought it secondhand from Philadelphia. It is estimated that 200 million gallons of water are lost in Boston through leaks. And cities and stated owed in 1988 close to $2 trillion! A rocky road is ahead.

PUBLIC SENTIMENTS ARE CHANGING

There seemed to be emerging some evidence of, and desire by, the public for a better quality of life, a decreased emphasis on material goals, the virtue of working for profit, the rightness of unqualified economic growth...and a concurrent rise in spiritual and humane values. This was seen in a growing migration of the middle-class from the suburbs to small towns farther away from everything. The economic implications of this move are profound: most of the $1.5 trillion in residential mortgage debt was in the suburbs, so any downturn in real estate prices, and large losses were bound to emerge.

But historically, this deep seated change in all of us is a cyclical rhythm of historical evolution, a Sigmoid type curve event described earlier, and it has operated all through recorded history with unfailing regularity. The questions arise: Must we go through a long period of human tragedy, trouble and want, the up-down phases common to past cultures in order to find a new and better way?

There is a great deal of evidence from history that we are in the early stages of an extraordinary downpath, a millennium cycle downturn of 500 years similar to that that happened in 1300 when the Black Death struck Europe and 40% of the population died in just four years. Or, perhaps a change as massive as that from the Middle Ages to the Industrial Revolution.[7]

The savage decline in the American dreams and destiny at this time, and the human tragedy and public anarchy that will ride along with it, could give birth to a modern dictator. Certainly the stage is set, as it was for other countries over long spans of history...Germany and Hitler, Italy and Mussolini, etc.

THE SECOND COMING AHEAD?

Is a Second Coming in our future? Will an Age of Benevolence similar to the Phoenix of Egyptian mythology, a bird that consumed itself by fire and after five hundred years rose from its ashes. Symbolically this represented a rebirth, a renewal of life, a resurrection of Truth, a symbol of life eternal, a new age of awareness, an eternal peace. This may be our path.

The social philosophy of tomorrow cannot be discovered now. If we look backward over history, we can see how impossible it is to stand in one age and predict the social philosophy of the next.

GOOD TIMES MUST ALWAYS END

At the turn of this century, Brooks Adams wrote a book entitled, *The Law of Civilization and Decay*. He developed a theory of history based on the idea that history is movement, moving over the long trend from barbarism to civilization.

Many of the things he wrote almost a century ago are common in our society today: the centralization of the public and power in large cities; economic competition was not beneficent—in the end it led always to degradation and the emergence of the money-lender; farm producers sink into debt; the division of the society into creditors and debtors; ultimately the public sinks deeper into debt which, with compound interest, can never be repaid; laws are designed to facilitate this—mortgage interest rate deduction on home loans, for example; finally, loans are made at soaring rates of interest—like credit card loans at 20 percent; the abundance of credit leads to speculation in real estate, the exchanges, and so on; finally, prices fall and bring ruin as the credit system falls apart.

This turning point in economic systems leads to political change. There is now a conflict between capital and labor. The historic solution to that has been "anarchy." It ends finally, then the entire system changes—political, social, cultural, economic. That sequence of events has started, and tomorrow will be very different for all of us.

Brooks Adams' conclusion in 1900 was much the same as mine is now. He wrote, "Anarchy, not collectivism, would be the outcome of the conflict between capital and labor."

The crushing depression of the 1930s did not produce anarchy, though there was a spirit of it. But now the bitter lines are drawn between capital (lenders) and labor (debtors), and they are too severe for the settlement to proceed much further amicably.

In addition, this time around, unique in all of U.S. history, the rich and ruling class loaned not only the public's resources to Latin nations who were bound to default, but they also loaned their own capital. For the first time they will take large losses instead of making large gains by buying things at low prices, like they did in the 1930s, when the Rockefellers built Rockefeller Plaza, for example, and when land prices had hit bottom.

So, the stage has been set for tumultuous change and the vanishing of all that now seems so familiar. The change now will permeate every nook and cranny of our society and our lives. Truly an upheaval is under way—not tomorrow, but now.

THE TIDES OF CHANGE

When Oswald Spengler wrote the *Decline of the West*, he accurately prophesied much of what has happened since in the industrial West.[8] Like Jeremiah, his warnings were disliked and unheeded. He said, essentially, that the West (back then) had to choose between which cultural community it wanted to follow: the laissez faire spirit of England and America, or the civil servant spirit of Prussia. He speculated that the West would fall under Anglo-American hegemony, which it has. He thought the following would result:

1) The world would be ravaged and exploited by rapacious plutocrats. These men would not rest until every section of the world had been industrialized for profit and more money.

2) The project would be mainly carried out by Americans since they had the largest natural reservoirs.

3) This would bring the rise of materialism to its most frightening form.

4) The final goal would be the creation of private wealth; the elimination of competition; the exploitation of the public through advertising; monetary influenced politics; the stimulation of false needs, and control of supply and demand.

Spengler also believed every declining civilization would see the coming of socialism in one form or another. He believed that in the West there were two forms of socialism: 1) an expression of the will of the masses, and 2) an expression of the spirit of order and discipline. This same idea was developed by H. G. Wells who called it "a community of will and a community of obedience."

The spirit of individualism which we place on a pedestal in America, has led to sharp social exploitations which are calculated mainly in money economic terms: the rich and the poor. But, is it better to judge people by the amount of money they possess or by their contribution to the State and through it to other people, a more human society? Would it not be better, therefore, to turn everyone into a civil servant so that we each have a stake in our own communities? The rich serve their nations, but primarily themselves since their lust for booty is the basic goal. As the Bible reminds us, *"Those who love money can never have enough."*

The important message of this book is that America is probably in a long historic decline. Americans have not noticed it because most often change is ignored by those in the middle of it—we prefer to keep our heads in the sands, to do our jobs each day and let someone else run the world. But by the late 1980s, the United States was in deep trouble. The entire infrastructure (our sewers, bridges, schools, prisons, etc.) were falling apart under our wall-eyed stare. For example, the *San Francisco Chronicle* reported May 7, 1988, that their entire 65,000 child school system was in a state of gross disrepair, with leaking school roofs, walls wrecked by neglect, desks destroyed, etc. The *Los Angeles Times* reported October 9, 1989 that New York City's infrastructure was literally collapsing.

Nothing will run as well tomorrow as we are used to seeing it run in our recent past. There will be more power blackouts and computer outages, telephone service will deteriorate, roads will fall apart, etc. This has already started: the *Los Angeles Times* reported October 9, 1989 that in New York City, "Over the last seven weeks, three different underground steampipes have exploded in Manhattan, spewing cancer-causing asbestos insulation over streets and buildings, shutting down businesses and—in the most serious instance—killing three people and forcing hundreds of families out of their apartments." They estimated 100,000 defects a year were reported, and it would take $50 billion to repair the infrastructure of New York City alone. Where will the funds come from in hard times to finance all of this when America is no longer creditworthy and can't borrow? Much of the trouble in Manhattan has been attributed to their financial crisis in the early 1970s when, to cut costs, repairs were abandoned.

SIGMOID CURVES OF CHANGE

The shape of the Sigmoid curve is generally thought of as a slanting "S" curve, and the lines of it, shown below, depict not only a law of nature but much else—a general pattern of change.

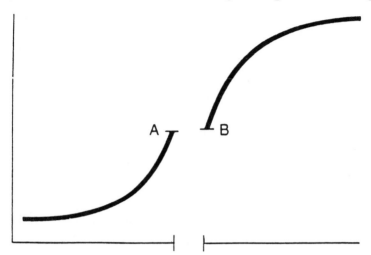

The rising Slope A is most familiar to Americans: a period marked by rapid economic change which is familiar to all of us: marked growth in population, use of energy, automobiles, technology, cities, suburbs, air transport, all accompanied by changing attitudes, values and behavior. Of course, there was the dark moral side: growth in crime, teenage abortions, growing prison populations, breakdowns of every imaginable sort in medical care systems, electronic systems, computer failures, power outages, and so on. It seemed endless.

The decay is a lot more extensive than in just the infrastructure. Our technological systems are in crisis: crisis in the welfare systems; crisis in the postal systems; crisis in the school systems; crisis in the health delivery systems; crisis in the urban systems; crisis in the financial system. The nation-state itself is in crisis. Our whole value system is in crisis.

We can all agree that we live with a great deal of economic

uncertainty these days. But we also face other challenges that will greatly affect our future. Some can foresee the possibility of a planet stripped of its resources and choked with pollution. Those scientists foresee unparalleled times of gut-wrenching decisions for a generation that has instinctively sought the "easy way" out. These "cynics" warn that unless we learn to deal with the problems we face on earth, we might not make it to the stars.

Why do we have the decay now on such a grand scale in America (wherever you turn you see this wreckage) after 300 years of successful industrial capitalism with its concomitant growth and prosperity and good times? Is it because of the Sigmoid curve effect? Nature—where everything grows old and dies? What?

I believe it to be our underestimating the power of nature and its rhythm. We also ignored history, but that is the nature of history…it is there to be ignored!

NO EASY TRANSITION

Can we repair the wrecked systems and simply go on? Or will decay bring in its wake violent change, of all sorts, that demands an upheaval, a new start?

I believe the transition period we are now in will be very painful: the cities will be ruled by gangs for awhile, breakdowns in distribution and communications will be commonplace (grocery store shelves will be empty, no gasoline, the phones won't work from time to time, for example), and repairing breakdowns will be very difficult if not impossible, social disruptions and riots in the streets, and so on. Why must this be?

Looking at the shape of Epoch A, it is safe to assume that to someone born in that period the future would appear to be unlimited in terms of growth and expansion: population, energy, agriculture, etc. But if you were born in Epoch B, the future would be a time of limitations with a ceiling on growth and expansion. It is obvious that a substantive qualitative difference emerges between A and B.

In Epoch A an increase in population was positive, but as we enter Epoch B it will be negative. Families were encouraged in A, and will be discouraged in B. In A, the industries that grew the most rapidly tended to dominate. This was evidenced in the period of exploration and colonization in the 17th, 18th and 19th centuries with the development of the industrial society. Growth was the dominant influence in social and economic life. Surely it has dominated the minds of our modern politicians and economists. They talk and think only in terms of "growth."

CHAPTER SIX

REFERENCES

1. *Los Angeles Times,* March 5, 1990.

2. Berle, Adolph A., *Power Without Property* (Harcourt, Brace & World, Harvest Book, N.Y.C., 1959).

3. Aaron & Bendiner, *The Strenuous Decade* (Doubleday, N.Y.C., 1970), p. 3.

4. Gimpel, Jean, *The Medieval Machine* (Halt, Rinehart & Winston, N.Y.C., 1976).

5. MaCauley, Lord, *Life and Letters of Lord MaCauley,* Trevelyn, Appendix, p. 405.

6. Wecter, Dicton, *The Age of the Great Depression* (Univ. of California Press, 1976).

7. The Millenium Cycle data is courtesy of Walter Studnicki, Scottsdale, Arizona.

8. Spengler, Oswald, *The Decline of the West* (Alfred A. Knopf, N.Y.C., 1926).

CHAPTER SEVEN

THE LONG HISTORICAL CYCLES

Life in the electronic age has divorced the public from any thought or feeling about the long cycles of economic and business activity. Television and radio have created "sound bite" news—fifteen seconds of information and that's it.

We have, because of this incessant conditioning, forgotten that cycles are ever present in our lives, in nature, they govern the tides and the moon.... Forgotten, and our emphasis and thinking is lodged with the short-lived activities which are so predominant.

But all through world history long cycles have existed. In the 1980s attention was drawn to the Kondratieff cycle, a business cycled discovered by a Russian economist. It stated that economic trends last from about 54 to 60 years from peak to peak, or trough to trough—about two generations in length. For example, this theory had it that the 1929 Crash on Wall Street was simply a turning point in this cycle, the upward phase of which had started in 1896, then turned down violently in the Crash of 1929.

But there are other significant cycles in the long records of history, and they have been given many titles, but "The Millennium Cycle" has been the one most often used to describe it. This being the turns that occur, roughly, in 1,000 year cycles. This chart depicts the ups and downs of this cycle:

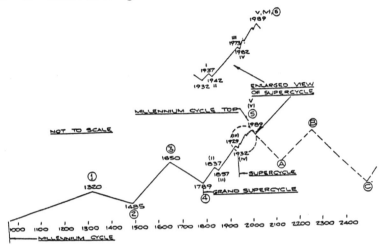

After the Roman Empire collapsed with its political and military structure, the world entered what could be called "The Age of Religion." The Roman Empire ceased to rule, but the Roman bishop remained, and the new Pope inherited the ceremonies, law, Latin language and costumes of the earlier era.

The Number 1 on the chart depicts the start of the "Millennium Wave." It was identified with the restoration of the Holy Roman Empire together with the advance of a combination of classical humanism and the Eastern mysticism in the Byzantine Empire. Virtually every ancient Green book known to us came through a Byzantine copyist. This first wave, Number 1, coincided with the revival of European cultural activity and the dominance of France throughout Europe. The Notre Dame cathedral in Paris was built then. It was also a time when optics, mathematics, and astronomy were developed. The systemizing of logic and dialectics emerged to facilitate intellectual inquiry.

During cycle Number 2 (1320 to 1485), the epidemic "Black Death" decimated populations in Italy, Spain, France, England and Germany, causing an estimated 40 percent fall in population. If that was not tragic enough, the "Hundred Years War" (1337 to 1453) destroyed the peasant population of France.

Wave Number 3 started in 1485 and it marked the transition

from medieval times to the modern way of life. Science-oriented philosophers started to replace scholasticism. The growth of finance, commerce and industry began in earnest to compete with the dominance of agriculture. This period also saw the emergence of the Renaissance, the Reformation, and reaction against the doctrinaire teachings of the Church. It was the twilight of the Era of Religion. Then came the discovery of America in 1492, the Great New Frontier, and soon, the emergence of the Era of Politics—a time familiar to all Americans.

In the next cycle, Number 4, the eruption of persecution for witchcraft, fanaticism, the Inquisition, and economic depression reigned.

Cycle Number 5 started after the American Revolution, the American Constitution, and George Washington. During this period there was a surge in interest and development in music, art, literature and the rapid growth of physics and geological sciences in the 20th century.

The chart now brings us up to the present Cycle. We have reached a top and are commencing a decline of immense proportions. Societies globally will ratchet down for hundreds of years, and bottoming out like Cycle Number 3 did, at level in our economy where we were in 1789.

The ongoing events since the Crash of late 1989 will intensify as America and the world accelerate into the longest and most severe Depression ever. It will mark the start of an Epic Transformation. All that was familiar in our past will transform: culture, politics, social structure, and money forms.

The downwave will, as all cycles do, have upturns, but they will be relatively brief and unrewarding. The optimism so natural to the American psyche will also vanish. The lower standard of living will, in its early stages, be hard to cope with, but later generations will accept life as it comes along and not fret over the past, but plan for a more austere tomorrow.

SLOW CYCLES

Why could we not have known about this before, and got ourselves prepared? This is because these long-term devastating cycles are barely visible in our every day lives, but plod on in the same direction, and the trend is a cumulative process which builds on its own achievements...it makes prices for the things we buy in our economic lives rise for long periods, then reaches a turning point when, with equal obstinacy, it begins working to bring prices down again over a longer period. Year by year the forceful trend cannot be seen but over centuries it is an event of great importance—as we are now discovering.

This long trend ferries along with it other cycles which have neither its longevity, serenity, or unobtrusiveness. These shoot up and down, and easy, indeed conspicuous to see. Every day life, today as in the past, is punctuated by these short-lived movements which must be added to the trend in order to estimate the whole. In our time these aberrations gained prominence as the media and the public, in turn, reacted to every miniscule bit of news about economic activity: Gross National Product estimates, employment data, home sales, car sales, and so on. All trivial, all sound-bite-type relevant in our recent past. And, now so far away from the reality we are all experiencing in our economic and financial lives.

Now all the foundations of economic life and all the lessons of our experience past and present are being challenged. And any attempt to explain "why" this is happening now seem impossible. Destiny? Who knows?

The crisis we are now in has always in history marked the process of destruction: our coherent world system which has developed at a leisurely pace since 1945 is going into a savage decline, one with no historical precedent for its steepness and anger.

This break with the past is a result of an accumulation of accidents, breakdowns and distortions. With the present persistent downward trend, the scene changes: global trade relations become touchy, social unrest diverts attention; the false standard of living to Third World levels for the highly industrialized nations present problems on an enormous scale, problems that seem now almost impossible to solve. But this phenomena has happened before, and populations have weathered the other storms.

WHAT HISTORY HAS TAUGHT US

The present global downturn compels that we look to history to find out what has happened to all of us and why. History's lessons include:

1) Societies move from being spread out all over a nation to concentrated in cities.
2) As old as historic time is the emergence of two conspicuous forms of thought: greed in good times, fear in hard times.
3) Growing competition among traders leaves in its wake, always, the usurer, always formidable, and the public, everyone else, and the history-old spread between the lives of the creditor and those of the debtor.
4) The division into creditors and debtors intensifies as concentration intensifies. Initially, the power of the creditor increases. As time goes on, however, the debtor finally rises to the top because the general public cannot repay the debt loads that always cripple them. The compound interest force always at work insures a financial collapse.
5) To keep debt growing (since credit/debt money is the money), Congress continually designs laws to encourage the public to go into debt—interest deductions on home mortgages, for example—and make it ever more profitable for the lender.
6) Finally, to keep the economic game going, loans are

made at interest rates so high that insolvency is certain to follow—credit card rates typify this; at rates of 20 percent, doubling the due sum every 3.5 years means few can repay.

7) As the credit base expands into "good times"—a byproduct of cheap credit—the speculator is reborn and he works not only on Wall Street but wherever he can borrow: autos, homes, corporate mergers, etc.

8) Finally, prices begin to fall again—as they started to do globally for raw materials as far back as 1973—and the decline goes far and is so devastating that debtors are ruined—as U.S. farmers have been in recent years, for example. This is because the debts assumed when prices were high cannot be repaid out of cash flows that come from lower prices.

9) At long last we discover in America that a very small role is played by conscious thought. These events have happened routinely all through recorded history almost as though they were predestined. We repeat the same human mistakes, as the Bible intones, over and over, so perhaps there is "nothing new under the sun." (Ecclesiastes 1:9)

CHAPTER EIGHT

THE SIZE OF UNCLE SAM'S DEBTS

Public debts go far back in history to the earliest times. In France and England, through many regimes and many rulers, public debt loomed large, and every time someone suggested its end, he was ousted. Napoleon was unique. He told his first cabinet council, "I will pay cash or nothing."

But early economists, such as Hume, viewed public debts as evil, believing that a nation no less than an individual should earn its money before spending it. But in our time, in a modern banker-economy, economists are pretty nearly unanimous in declaring that the manipulation of public credit, when "wisely done" and "within certain bounds," is a blessing, and that it may even account for the great advance in human comfort and happiness in the past two hundred years. It is also observed that at the very stage of the growth in public debt, those fearful of this growth have continuously predicted that ruin and bankruptcy were near. For example, when William Pitt ran the debt of Britain to 140 million pounds; and again when the debt reached 800 million pounds; and then when it reached a billion, men were certain it could never be paid. Yet Britain grew more and more prosperous all the time. The same increase of wealth, coincident with the increase in public debt, has been noted, with great joy, in America by all of our leading politicians and economists.

The economists tell us that the benefits that flow from debt include the lessons we are taught to work harder, to keep up the payments, and that business thrives by debt, not thrift.

But those who cherish the notion of public borrowing as a stimulus to wealth nearly always draw all of their conclusions from the experiences of just two nations: Great Britain and the United States of America. But this choice is made of the two nations that have progressed fastest and farthest in the last two hundred years. It was done during the age of the great industrial and trading era, and when the native genius of the people easily adapted to this new order.

But there is always one point never mentioned: the British public debt cost that nation the American colonies. It was not the hardness of heart that brought the American Revolution. It was, instead, the natural (though fatal) desire of Britain to pass part of the debt-service burden on to the colonies, and the equally natural refusal of the Americans to support the burden which they had not willingly assumed.

The case of the United States is a marvel in colonization and development which has no parallel in the world's history. Nowhere was there ever such a body of land to be exploited, never anywhere an immigration with such a genius for tapping those hidden riches. So rapid was the production of wealth, even with temporary setbacks of wars, or speculation-madness, that the United States could, during most of its life, have borne a much larger public debt that it did, had it been necessary.

But the public borrowing of all other nations tells a different story. If we go beyond Great Britain and the United States (neither of which, as a nation, has ever defaulted its public debts), we cruise into a turbulent sea of defaults, repudiations, litigations, compositions, refundings, forced settlements, swindles, inflations, and political jobbery that sickens the soul. Not that some other nations have been without their periods of perfect rectitude and sound financing. But the trusting creditors, everywhere else, at one time or another, by one means or another, have been caught, thrown, and sheared.

IN OUR TIME: CANADIAN PUBLIC DEBTS

By early 1990, the per capita public debt level in Canada had risen above that of the United States. And then came the bad news: the Canadian Bond Rating Service "warned that the Canadian government's ability to maintain its top-ranked triple-A credit rating is under great pressure because of mounting debt." The agency went on to say, "That the government's financial position is considerably weaker today than it was at the beginning of the 1981-82 recession." [1]

Does the weakness in Canadian public debt portend similar problems and loss of creditworthiness by the American government, whose debts loads are positively enormous? The sense of this book, as you will read, is that this may be now unavoidable for America. A day of reckoning could be nearing for all of us.

NEXT: AMERICAN "RISKY" PUBLIC DEBTS

By late 1989 warnings of trouble with the Federal government's growing financial problems were made public by the Comptroller General who stated that "the money being lost annually to fraud, waste and mismanagement could total $150 billion." [2] Beyond that, the Office of Management and Budget had made a list of 73 federal programs that posed a financial risk to the taxpayer. The total risk amounted to hundreds of billions of dollars. The OMB Director called this "Hidden Pacmen that are waiting to spring forward and consume another line of resource dots in the budget maze." Various Senate committees then began to prepare lists of "high-risk" federal programs with financial programs and troubles that had long gone uncorrected.

Among the "high-risk" programs were many of the Federal government agencies listed on page 99. Foremost, in early 1990, were the signs of the growing failure of the Resolution Trust Corporation, which as formed to save the savings and loan industry. It was funded at the outset with $50 billion and as time went on more and more requests were made for additional borrowed funds since future loan losses had been grossly under-estimated. No one could guess by early 1990 how high the risk was for just that one "rescue." But *Barron's* magazine estimated it to be closer to $900 billion than $100 billion.[3]

The high risk agency that would hit the public where it would hurt the most—in its pocketbook—was the Federal Deposit Insurance Corporation insuring bank accounts—a federal agency with $14 billion in reserves to fund $1.8 trillion in bank deposit exposure—a marvelous example of leverage at work. The public believed that if a bank run were to happen, the government would raise the shortfall with taxes or by borrowing more, if it could, and then retrieving these resources later from consumers by taxing. The public seemed to believe this, since there was no visible public concern in 1990 about the safety of their own monies in the banks. However, if the government had had to do that, then it would bring on major financial problems from another source: overtaxed taxpayers paying new taxes would then be short of funds to repay their own enormous debts, thus precipitating a financial crisis in that sector.

So, by early 1990 the debt chickens of Uncle Sam were coming home to roost. Starkly, as the problems grew, warnings began to emerge, but public confidence in the ability of the federal government to solve the mountain of problems remained high.

The strong public confidence was a carryover of two generations of public belief that the government could solve any problem. They believed, for example, that Social Security checks were still on time as proof, and words of confidence from politicians continued. Beyond all of that, the public was still heavily involved in their own consumption—and their own personal debt problems this pattern had created.

It is amazing that those politicians who marvel at the virtues of frugality and thrift, so much esteemed by the individual, should not carry those same ideas forward into public officialdom and help to implement them. Especially since 1980 in America we have seen the extraordinary expansion of public debts. We were told that this is "good," that we must spend vast sums of borrowed money to defend America, that we can afford it, that the debt load is tolerable because we owe it to ourselves. So, dollars are really just changing hands, and in real dollars after inflation, it is not that big and, therefore, not troublesome. Most of these arguments are proposed by our modern economists who, by training, see nothing wrong with debt. They are the same ones that believe "liquidity" is to add more debt to the current debt loads. They also seem to be oblivious of the extraordinary power of compound interest. This is a paradox, because they, of all people, as mathematicians, should know better than the rest of us its inevitable future wrecking power.

But the assumption that government debt can be constantly extended, implies a belief in constant growth of wealth to infinity. In other words, so far as we know nature, it is based on a transparent fallacy.

The burden of debt, public and private, constitute a grave danger to our health, safety and welfare than all the nuclear bombs stockpiled in America.

It is the argument of this book that here is the reality: our Mother-Lode-free-resource discoveries since 1492 are nearly all exhausted and the economic growth in America by exploiting these free resources has ended; the by-products of industrial growth in the destruction of the environment, the air, the water, and so on, are also ruining our lives and land space and must end; our mammoth public debts without parallel for any nation in all of recorded economic history, with interest compounded at the high rates now prevalent, insure that the American public debts can probably never be repaid.

If so, then the future promises tumultuous change in our lives and in the future for America and the way we have lived and will live in the future.

DEFICITS AND PUBLIC DEBT

For years the American public has been promised a balanced federal budget which has rarely been delivered by Congress. The consequences of continuing deficits and growing federal debts at compound rates of interest are a mystery to the average man. Some of it lies in the distinction between the budget, which is widely reported by the media, and the actual receipts and expenditures of the federal government, which is not so widely reported. The latter is what counts over the long run.

The federal budget is very little different from a family budget. It is a plan of listing income and expenses and, hopefully, the first exceeds the second. If not, adjustments are made: either you must increase the income or cut your expenses. What really counts over time in our budgets, however, is what we actually receive and what we actually spend. That is what determines the real deficit or surplus. This is also true for the government. But politicians rarely follow the rigid rules of income and outgo. For example, in devising the Gramm-Rudman plan in the 1980s, which required that the budget deficit be gradually reduced to zero by 1993, Congress limited the deficits up until then to certain numbers. But in the real world spending continually increased, as it has for years.

So, the question arises, how can Congress legislate a budget with reduced deficits and continue to spend more than they take in? Easy. They simply do not include some expenses in the budget that should be there. And they also include some expenses in the budget that should be there. And they also include some income that should *not* be there. In late 1980, several hundred billions of dollars that will ultimately be spent on the savings and loan industry rescue were not included in the federal budget in order to reduce expenses. The Postal Service was removed from the budget so its losses would not be revealed. Social Security tax receipts which are mandated by law to go into a separate trust fund are included in the budget to increase income. Congress has the authority to include or exclude whatever it wants, and it also has the ability to spend money that does not have to be reported in the budget. So, the Gramm-Rudman targets were easily met. And the deficits report to the public were not the real deficits. What they reveal is irrelevant; what really matters is what is the actual spending?

When Congress spends money, it can get it, in the narrow sense, in one of two ways: it can tax, or it can borrow. Congress cannot create money as so many people believe. The Federal Reserve can only create bank reserves through the banking system after the Treasury has created debt in the form of securities. The Federal Reserve does not have the power to create this debt, which is another widely held myth. It is the buying and selling of these Treasury debt securities that increase or decrease bank reserves and allows banks to make loans to the government. The new loans are money, but that is also an idea not well understood. The public thinks money is *paper money,* Federal Reserve Notes, which really only make up less than 5% of all the so-called "money." The rest is credit money, credits that come into being when a loan is made, when money is borrowed. Our society runs on borrowed money, loans, debt. That is the problem, of course: too much debt all over America.

Raising taxes does not increase the deficit. In the short run it lowers the deficit. But the greater danger now with a tax increase is that if one were put in place, then consumers would be deprived of that income to pay their own $3 trillion in debts, so a tax raise could precipitate consumer debt defaults on a large scale, and create havoc—even financial doomsday—in the economy.

So, the item that is left that increases the deficit is *more borrowing by Uncle Sam.* When Congress must borrow more it simply means that they have spent more than they took in. and the dollar amount of the borrowing tells us exactly how much that was. So, if you want to determine what the real deficit is, you must look at the dollar amount the federal debt increased, not the deficit reported in the budget. For example, on April 12, 1989, the total federal debt was $2,755 million. Eight months later, on January 8, 1990, the total federal debt had risen to $2,941 million. This was a rise of $186 billion, which amounted to $20.6 billion a month. If that figure were annualized it would equal $247.2 billion a year in new debt, which equals $4.7 billion a week.[4]

The gross federal debt at the end of fiscal 1986 was $2,110 billion; at the end of 1987 it had increased to $2,355 billion, a jump of $225 billion, which was truly the real deficit. At the end of fiscal 1988 the gross debt level was $2,615 billions, an increase of $259 billion. By the end of 1989 it had risen to $2,881 billion, another increase of $267 billion. The reported deficit for 1989 was $159 billion, a discrepancy of 68%.

The deficits of Uncle Sam are, then, much worse than the public thinks they are, and why they are also ignored by the public.

WHY MORE DEBTS?

Congress must continually expand the national debt base because national prosperity, the briskness of trade and profits all depend on debt expansion. This is because debt is the money supply and more money in the economic system generates good times.

The federal debt has been increasing every year and this means that all existing debt must be continuously exchanged, or rolled over, as this process is called. In other words, as each batch of Treasury Bill or Treasury Bonds fall due, the Department of the Treasury must not only borrow the money to pay it off, but must also borrow at the same time more to finance the continuing deficit spending.

Since the average maturity of all federal debts has now fallen to 4-1/2 years, the size of the refunds have become rapid and enormous, bordering on absurdity. For example, on March 2,

1990 the Treasury had to sell $16 billion in short-term bills (52-day cash management bills) to redeem $15.5 billion in maturing bills, plus allowing them an extra $750 million in cash. This offering was dated March 5 and would mature April 26, 1990.[5] The minimum purchase was $1 million and they were sold through the Federal Reserve Banks.

UNCLE SAM PAYS TOP DOLLAR

Since the government has no choice but to borrow, it must borrow and pay whatever rate of interest it has to. It is not limited as you and I would be by the interest expense. It can borrow and ignore that cost. If it did not do this, it would face default. If it defaulted it could not borrow a nickel from anyone from then on. Holders of Treasury Debts would also lose.

GROWING LIKE TOPSY

The debt has increased 182% since 1980, while the means to repay it (the Gross National Product, where wealth is created in making goods and services) has grown only 76%. Debt levels have grown more than twice as fast as the means to repay them.

In 1960 only 10% of the budget went to pay interest costs. By 1975 this had risen to 13%, and by 1989 it was over 19%. This means that the increase in the federal debt between 1980 and the present was so great that the portion of the budget going to pay the interest expense on that debt not only increased from 13% to just over 19%, but happened while interest rates were in a brief decline from their super-high level of 18% in 1980 to 8.5% in 1990. But interest rates have since started to rise again.

Because of interest compounding at a steady rate of 8%, one day not far off the total interest would exceed the GNP. At 8% the total dollars double every nine years. This means that by 1999 the total federal debts, documented below, will have increased from $11 trillion to $22 trillion.

The government's demand for funds will steadily increase in the future mainly because of this interest growth, even if spending was reduced. This ongoing demand can only be met with higher interest rates and, some day, the sums could be so large as to swamp the domestic markets. The vicious circle goes like this: the government will pay whatever it must to borrow, and paying higher rates means the federal interest expense increases rapidly; this increase then raises the deficit which means more borrowing must be done, and this extra demand increases the rates again, and on and on. It all goes on automatic pilot sooner rather than later.

The size of the federal government's total exposure to debts by this borrowing process has rocket to record levels since 1980. The government has also steadily taken on an extraordinary amount of financial risk through a wide variety of loan guarantees, insurances, etc., such as pension plan insurance, mortgage insurances, farm credit insurance, etc.

If the enormous debt level is not high enough, it *is also highly leveraged.* Leveraged debt carries with it great risk since any downturn in tax revenues for Uncle Sam, for example, means an immediate rise in debts and borrowing must increase to meet the tax shortfall. Government exposure on its bank deposits is a classic case of leverage: the FDIC insurance fund in 1990 had about eight-tenths of one cent for every $1 on deposit. Thus, if there is a bank run on the $1+ trillion in bank deposits, the shortfall between government bank insurance and risk-exposure could only be met by more borrowing. But, this would come at a time when it would be risky for Uncle Sam, thus forcing the government to pay high rates of interest, adding to its total debt load and worsening the central problem: too much debt already at high rates of interest. It is this debt phenomenon, as it was in France before Napoleon, that led to debt repudiation there.

If this leveraged debt was not bad enough, the government, like any large lender, was in the late 1980s also suffering large losses from bad debts. By the end of 1989, government receivables totalled $540 billion, of which $168 billion were delinquent. As these delinquent accounts increase and the government's contingent liabilities, listed below, fall due, then the enormous deficits will probably increase still more.

Increasingly, it appeared in 1990 that the government's risky debt exposure could only get worse. The current savage economic downturn will simply worsen the position of our largest debtor as tax revenues decline and unemployment and welfare costs rise to unparalleled heights and widening the deficits to over $400 billion a year.

In 1972, the government's liabilities were $1.4 trillion. At the end of 1989 they were over $10 trillion. Here is the breakdown, which is larger than that reported by the General Accounting Office, noted on page 96, probably because more potential liability threats are in $10 trillion estimate. At any rate, here is a resume of the liabilities and, though long, probably is not 100% complete:

PRIVATE LOAN GUARANTEES

	(Billions)
Federal Home Loan Banks	$143.5
Federal Home Loan Mortgage Corp.	26.7
Federal National Mortgage Association	111.5
Farm Credit Banks	58.5
Student Loan Mortgage Association	27.1
Financing Corporation	8.1
Farm Credit Financial Assistance Corp.	1.0
Rural Housing Insurance Fund	20.7
Federal Ship Financing Fund	12.6
Export Import Bank Loans	11.8
Rural Development Insurance fund	7.8
Medical Facilities Guarantee Fund	5.6
Foreign Military Sales	24.2
Pension Benefit Guarantee Corp.	800.0

Multilateral Development Trust	28.0
Other	25.0
	TOTAL $1,333.7

INSURANCE LIABILITIES (Billions)

Bank Deposit Insurance	$2,142.0
S&L Deposit Insurance	964.0
Credit Union Insurance	180.0
Farmer's Home Administration	800.0
Securities Investor Protection Corp.	1.0
Riot Insurance	809.0
Nuclear Regulatory Insurance	138.6
Veterans Life Insurance	45.9
Ocean Shipping War Risk Insurance	10.0
Flood Insurance	48.2
Overseas Private Investment Insurance	10.2
Others	20.2
	TOTAL $5,167.3

SOCIAL SECURITY (Billions)

Unfunded Liability in Trust Funds	$4,026.0

OTHER PENSION, COMPENSATION FUNDS

(Billions)

Veterans	$ 85.2
Military Retirement	201.2
Civil Service	142.1
Additional Acturarial Deficits	27.2
	TOTAL $455.7

INTERNATIONAL AND OTHER LIABILITIES

(Billions)

Pledges to World Bank and Other Organizations	$ 35.6
Unsettled Claims	22.1
Other Contingencies	41.2
	———
TOTAL	$ 98.9

GRAND TOTAL: $11,087.6 billion

This vast sum does not include direct debt of the government and its agencies, now more than $3 trillion.

Sources: Federal Reserve Bulletin, various issues; Treasury Bulletin, various issues 1989; 1990 Budget Documents.

WHAT ARE THE RISKS?

There are risks attendant with this vast liability exposure, and they include: 1) The reality that tax receipts can in no way redeem most of these debts without the sale of more debt, 2) The risk of the $9 trillion in privately held debt in America (consumers, corporations and cities and states)—and, the unraveling of that debt would diminish tax receipts sharply, worsening the plight of the federal government, 3) The price deflation the economy is in now means less cash flow for everyone with which to pay off debts incurred when cash flows were high, 4) The falling dollar abroad making U.S. Treasury debt obligations less inviting to foreign investors, 5) The net debtor position of the U.S. to the world as domestic trade deficits have displayed for many years.

Any and all of these conditions magnify the risk problems of the federal government.

WOULD THE GOVERNMENT RENEGE ON ITS DEBTS?

Would you believe the U.S. Government has a past history of repudiating its debts? After the Revolutionary War, debts were paid off with worthless currency (The "Continental"). On May 2, 1933, the government revised the terms of payment on its debts in a manner that was bad for debt owners. On that date, obligations of the United States were offered with the explicit guarantee that interest and principal would be made in Gold Dollars, the Gold Dollar being defined as equal to 25.802 ounces of gold. But on June 5, 1933, a Joint Resolution of Congress declared such contracts to pay Gold Dollars void and unenforceable. That declaration was upheld by the Supreme Court in February 1935.

There is, of course, no guarantee that the government will not somehow revise the terms of its covenants with bondholders and other creditors to the disadvantage of the owners.

But, it is the argument of this book that that event might not happen because there is a chance a convergence of future financial, political and social events could force the repudiation of debts by the government.

Such an event could be precipitated by private sector debt liquidation soon to start in our economy, thus reducing tax revenues and sending government deficits into the heavens. This would be coupled by the recognition of this domestic financial catastrophe by foreign debt owners, compelling them to cash in.

The next chapter outlines the possibility that national bankruptcy may be in our future. Who can know now?

Right or wrong, it only makes sense to prepare your own security—just in case.

CHAPTER EIGHT

REFERENCES

1. *Wall Street Journal*, February 27, 1990.

2. *Barron's*, March 5, 1990.

3. *Barron's*.

4. *Wall Street Journal*, January 24, 1990.

5. *Wall Street Journal*, February 28, 1990.

CHAPTER NINE

CAN WE FACE NATIONAL BANKRUPTCY IN AMERICA?

In Franklin Roosevelt's first press conference on March 8, 1933, he was asked about the country's plight after the dramatic closing of the banks, and specifically what he thought about the government guaranteeing bank deposits. He said, "The general underlying thought behind the use of the word 'guarantee' with respect to bank deposits is that you guarantee bad banks as well as good banks. The minute the government starts to do that the government runs into probable loss.... We all know it is better for a bank to take a loss than to jeopardize the credit of the United States Government."[1]

It was the sterling, unimpaired credit of the United States of America that provided the financial credits necessary to try and get the nation out of Great Depression I. The FRC, TVA, and other national agencies were easy to fund because Uncle Sam's credit was impeccable. In those days, borrowed funds were repaid out of the wealth they created.

FINANCIAL CRISIS

But it was the federal financial ideas created in the 1930s that are leading Americans to the coming national bankruptcy crisis. This is because all of the ideas for stirring the economy revolved around the creation of debt, and spending the credits so created. And interest-bearing debts to boot. And not, in this process, creating wealth to provide the means to repay the debts.

For years the borrowing process went on with what were apparently beneficent effects. There were no Depressions to follow, but the economy did have a number of recessions which varied in their intensity.

But the American national debt orgy of the early 1980s and the doubling of federal deficits (piled on top of years of federal borrowing), coupled with huge trade deficits and an exploding use of debt in the private sector, led to where we are now. America has a total domestic debt load of nearly $20 trillion ($11 trillion federal and $9 trillion private sector) and we do not have the resources to repay the obligations. We borrowed not to create wealth, but to juggle money since there was profit in that, as well.

FEDERAL DEBT TROUBLES

In the bitter end, the most troubling problem for all Americans will be the debt problems of the federal government. The reason they are so devastating is that all domestic credit rests on the sanctity of the credit of the federal government, or what is called "the full faith and credit" of the government. For example, the Federal Reserve issues paper money (Federal Reserve Notes) for use in the domestic money system. The collateral for these notes was, until the 1930s, gold. But then the collateral was changed to U.S. Treasury Bonds—one debt supporting another.

GOVERNMENT CREDIT IS MONEY NOW

By using Treasury Debt as collateral for paper money, the government substituted government credit for money instead of gold. And that substitution will prove to be fatal to our economy.

Now, if the federal government is forced into national bankruptcy, then the value of the government bonds will plummet and could even approach zero. Who knows? But in this process the value of paper money also disappears. The total amount of paper money outstanding is not large: on April 26, 1989, the total amount of paper money in circulation was only $216 billion.

Paper money is important psychologically to the public, however, since they are the main users of this currency and many believe it is the only currency. They have little idea that in our economy we use credit as a substitute for money since it, too, has purchasing power. The use of credit cards was thought of by the public as "different" and not "money." Money was paper and coins in their minds.

But far more important, and as fragile, are the paper instruments that represent wealth. These include mortgages on homes, car loan papers, etc. and, of course, the federal debt instruments: $2.7 trillion of "full faith and credit debt" (Treasury Bills, Bond Notes, and GNMAEs, all supported by taxpayer revenues), plus trillions of other federal guarantees on everything from bank deposits to mortgage repayments, to student loans being guaranteed by the federal government, and so on.

But in this vast trillions of dollars federal debt system, the only resource of the Federal Reserve System (the U.S. Central Bank) was about $250 billion in Treasury debt. But, what held the whole thing together was the belief and confidence in America, an implicit feeling that the federal government was "creditworthy."

As with any debtor, however, it is plain that excessive debt obligations that cannot be repaid, much less serviced, is the sure road to bankruptcy, whether it be the national government or a private individual or corporation. So, it was imperative that the government preserve its own creditworthiness.

Alas. The only way the government could raise funds was to borrow. As this process continued, it rapidly reached the stage where the process by itself was creating interest on interest at compound rates which rose faster than components of the Gross

National Product. This slowed economic growth and ultimately lead to government debt repayment problems. Insolvency. Default.

With any borrower, the more they borrow, the less chance they have to repay borrowed money unless incomes rise. But that was not happening in America in the late 1980s. The economy was slowing down, going first into recession, then depression, and then a period rapidly emerged where, to fund the problems of hard times, the government's borrowing needs soared. Deficits of $400 billion a year became commonplace as tax revenues plunged.

But this was not all that was happening: there were the other federal credit guarantees that were becoming unraveled. It started with the Savings and Loan crisis in 1988-1989, a crisis first estimated to cost $20 billion, then escalated to $400 billion.[2] There was truly no end in sight.

But that was not all: the government had insured banks and credit union deposits, too, about $1.5 trillion, plus mortgage guarantees of over $700 billion, and so on. These contingent liabilities ran into the trillions.

Beyond that, the federal government debt held by foreigners was nearly $300 billion—removing control of domestic debt problems from the hands of the government. At any time, there was the threat that foreigners would fear default, repudiation, or whatever, and sell their U.S. Treasury debts, thus destroying the U.S. bond markets where the bulk of the "paper wealth" was traded, and which was about three times larger than the stock market.

DEADLY DEFICITS

Back in 1986, the United States Government went into deficit for the fourth year in a row, and the deficit was about $200 billion for that one year alone. Beyond that admitted debt, over $15 billion a year was routinely funnelled through the enigmatic Federal Financing Bank (a creation of Congress to prevent debt disclosures and pave the way for off the budget financing).

Beyond that, the federal debt also grew about $5 billion more than acknowledged. So, it is safe to assume the $200 billion deficits will continue—until the present crisis makes them explode.

But one of the most insidious aspects of just a $200 billion deficit is that it will add tens of billions of dollars to every future year's deficit as well. This is because interest must be paid on this one year's deficit in every subsequent year. And not only that, because the interest adds to future years' deficits, interest must also be paid on the interest.

So the federal deficits compound in a geometric progression (2,4,8,16), growing and growing forever, even in the unlikely event that future budgets could be balanced—balanced, that is, except for interest.

For example, here is the consequence over the next ten years of the $200 billion fiscal 1986 deficit, assuming an otherwise balanced budget in all years subsequent to 1986 and an average interest rate of 8%:

Fiscal Year	Deficit (S Billions)	Interest on 1986 Deficit and Interest on Interest (S Billions)	Cumulative Cost (S Billions)
1986	S 200	- - -	S 200
1987	0	S 16	216
1988	0	17	233
1989	0	19	252
1990	0	20	272
1991	0	22	294
1992	0	23	317
1993	0	26	343
1994	0	27	370
1995	0	30	400
1996	0	32	432

This data clearly shows that a single $200 billion deficit will actually cost more than $400 billion within a decade, and the burden will keep on growing like that forever. In just 21 years, the $200 billion 1986 deficit alone, and the interest on it, will have cost more than $1,000 billion—one trillion dollars. That vast sum is the consequence of a single year's profligacy and is three times as great as the accumulated federal debt from the Revolutionary War through the War in Vietnam, a span of nearly two centuries.

If you think this is a foolish theory, look at budget proposals since 1986; for 1987 a total of $148 billion was slated to be spent on debt interest alone. By 1988 it was $169 billion just for interest.

In other words, past deficits directly account for all of the next year's deficit as projected at that time.

Now. We have growing federal deficits that can never be paid back. Our government, like all debtors, is on the road to national bankruptcy, and that is no exaggeration. Why must this be? Debts are always paid, remember—either the government collects enough taxes to pay the debts back or the debts must be declared "no good," thus destroying our national creditworthiness. It is as simple as that. Worse, the forces are irreversible.

What if the debts were just cancelled, as some propose? Then that would be the end of credit, so that is not a solution. The historic solution for many nations all through history was to go broke, then set in motion forces to start the financial machine up again.

This is why the future is so perilous for all Americans.

IN THE END, HYPERINFLATION?

It was widely believed by the public that debt liquidation and hard times to follow would not be the problem. It would instead be a hyperinflation, like that which occurred in Germany after World War I. Could that happen in America? No. Why not?

The main buyers of U.S. Government debts are banks, wealthy private individuals, insurance companies, Wall Street financial firms, etc. In fact, there are special securities firms on Wall Street who deal only in government debt, and it has always been assumed—until now—that there will always be a buyer for government debt. But that was not true in Germany any more than it will be true in America in the 1990s.

L. Albert Hahn wrote in *Economics of Illusion* on the German experience:[3]

"From the spring of 1922 on the following situation developed in Germany: the obligations of the government for new expenditures, as well as for the renewal of obligations coming due, were no longer purchased by the public and not even by banks. They had to be taken over by the central bank (The Reichsbank) against newly created paper money. Unlimited issuance of government obligations had undermined confidence in the currency so that no one was willing to retain his mark securities but purchased goods and foreign exchange. It was primarily this plethora of paper money, newly created to pay off maturing debt, which was the chief cause for the development of runaway inflation."

In the late 1980s, we saw that same phenomena in Argentina, Brazil, and Mexico. But they did not have bond markets, and the paper money was printed by the government to pay its bills and so fed through the public, causing prices to rise. Those who could, in those countries, also took their funds out in "capital flight" to preserve its purchasing power as they did in Germany.

The Federal Reserve system has the power to pay for newly issued debt by printing Federal Reserve Notes, instead of its long-term practice of paying by a check credit to the seller's account at his bank, creating more bank credits that way.

But that practice will fail because the character of money in America has changed. The American money system is not like the German system was, nor is it like the Argentine system in the late 1980s. Money in America has been transformed into computer money. This represents a quantum jump in how we think about money in this epic transformation from paper money to computer-electronic-money in the past fifteen years. This changed "money" for us, how we thought of it, and how it, in turn, changed our lives.

We have all had the personal experience of asking for our balances at a bank and waiting until the bank computer tells us how much money we have. It was this change that made possible electronic wire transfers of "money" in vast sums, trillions of dollars a day whirring around the world on computers. At any end of this practice, when the numbers showed up, the recipient was paid in cash, if he wanted, which few did, or by check (a credit) and used that form of money to spend—since computer money had purchasing power like other forms of bank credit money.

The computer money made possible credit cards and electronic wire transfers of money running into the trillions of dollars, and made our financial system run at an accelerating rate of credit-money-computer transfers.

NEW MONEY FORM

The nature of money in America has changed dramatically in the last sixty years. When money was commodity-based and bank demand deposits did not pay interest, money was fairly static. All of the price indexes were based on the notion that money was indeed static. The indexes could not gain or lose value unless there were changes in the money price of other assets. In the past it meant that the only way a saver could gain would be when real asset prices fell, that is, for there to be a price deflation. But in these times the character of savings is very different. Virtually all savings now are held in the form of interest-bearing liabilities of the banking system, and they no longer represent a withdrawal of money from circulation.

But these new savings have a cost and the cost is interest. When interest rates rise above the rate of creation of new credit, they reduce the amount of credit available for the wealth creating sector. This is because the payment of interest demands that much of new credits be siphoned off to pay this increased cost, thus making less net new credits available to the entire system. This new credit money diversion from wealth production to credit service cost creates an imbalance between the monetary and wealth producing sectors, finally reducing the ability to repay debts in any way because of this phenomena of servicing debts—there are fewer credits left to pay interest on debts.

So, money is no longer like monetary theories state—it is not what we think it is.

GLOBAL THREAT

The new form of credit money, that on a computer, and the U.S. position of having the dollar as the world reserve currency, made for the internationalization of the U.S. credit-dollar. "Good as gold," it was believed. Much of the world trade was denominated in dollars, including the price of oil. To a large part the world ran on U.S. credit.

WE REAP WHAT WE SOW

CHANGING THE RULES

Since the Federal Reserve System was organized in December 1913, its operations were defined by certain legal rules of order. Among its many powers was one that permitted it to be the American "bank of last resort." The meaning of this was that if any financial institution or large corporation got into credit problems, it was the function of the Federal Reserve to rescue it, like it did the Pennsylvania Railroad, the Chrysler Corporation, The Continental Bank, and others over the years.

DISCOUNT WINDOW

One of the main sources of credit from the Federal Reserve

was the use of its discount window. This meant, for example, that a bank having credit problems could present its inventory of Treasury debt to the branch of the Federal Reserve where it was located. The Federal Reserve Bank would then buy the paper back and calculate the purchase price of the paper at the face amount of the paper, less interest deducted (discounted) in advance.

Up until 1989, the Federal Reserve, like any banker, demanded only high quality paper for discount—generally Treasury debt or, in the early days, paper that was self-liquidating (paper whose proceeds would be liquidated by the loan). This kept the Federal Reserve central banking system liquid and the currency elastic—since the supply of goods was paid for by the proceeds.

This bond was broken in the 1930s when the Federal Reserve was allowed to discount government debt because those debts were not self-liquidating. This set the stage for banks and others to make long-term loans with their short-term deposits. "Borrowing short and lending long" this was called. No longer was debt maturity matched to deposit maturity. An illiquid society was in the making.

THE LAST STEP

Bad as this was, it became worse. On April 25, 1989, the *Wall Street Journal* reported, "The Federal Reserve Board, making good on its promise to be the lender of last resort for cash-starved savings and loans, was forced to open its discount window to Lincoln Savings and Loan last week." This was a revolutionary event.

As described, all through history, the Federal Reserve had been permitted to lend only to solvent institutions with good collateral. But Lincoln Savings had no collateral; as a matter of fact, the Federal Home Loan Bank of San Francisco had previously refused to lend to Lincoln Savings saying their paper was "useless."[4]

This almost unnoticed financial happening set the stage for the approaching national bankruptcy. It meant that if, as the financial crises worsened in the 1990s, any bank, thrift, or other financial institution that got into a credit crunch, a liquidity squeeze, a shortage of credit, etc., the Federal Reserve would advance the funds to save them—filling its role as the "lender of last resort."

As this process continued, the American Central Bank, the Federal Reserve, would undermine itself and make itself insolvent and not creditworthy. And take America down in that process.

The reason this will happen is that a bank must have A-1 collateral—some kind of collateral that could be sold if the loan turned bad. As consumers we have all had the experience of bankers asking and getting the best kind of collateral before making a loan.

WHAT DOES THIS MEAN?

When we live on credit beyond our means in America, the debt sooner or later overtakes us. If we tax ourselves to pay for our past debts, this means we all go back a little. If we repudiate debts, that is the end of credit. In this dilemma, the ideal solution recommended to us since the late 1930s, even to the creditor, was to issue more credit, more debt.

But the extension of credit is finite. Sooner or later the compounding interest payments on it will make it impossible to repay the principal, thus rendering the debt useless. The credit limit of the U.S. Government is just how much the government can tax the public to get income to pay back its debts. Since the government will rarely, if ever, do that, they will continue to borrow—as they are doing—and finance every shipwrecked bank, thrift, and corporation in the country, run up mammoth debts, and precipitate national bankruptcy.

THE WORST OF TIMES

In sum: as the Federal Reserve continued to advance funds

through the discount process, growing financial system failures were being created. The final consequences of this deadly practice, and root change in the basic rules of the game, would end in the Federal Reserve's collateral base rapidly moving from a liquid form of collateral that could be turned into cash quickly to an illiquid form of paper, where there would be no available liquidity to rescue bad advances, thus making the institution itself insolvent. The losses generated through this process by the Federal Reserve banking system would finally be transferred to the U.S. Treasury in the bitter end. Thus, national bankruptcy would be the certain and inevitable end of this fatal train of events.

THE CONSEQUENCES

The Federal Reserve Notes, our paper money, will then have no value. U.S. Treasury Debts would also lose their value. We will transform, as other nations have before us, into national bankruptcy with the public rooting through the ashes since all representations of wealth that they owned—mortgages, certificates of deposit, money market funds, etc.—would also have no value. We will be bankrupt as a nation and impoverished as citizens. There is no alternative, no nostrums, to change this hard reality. But this does not mean that we will not be told that there are solutions.

Answers galore will be promised, and the worse things get, the more promises that will be made to the public.

Then one day, out of a clear blue sky, lightning will strike: foreign holders of U.S. dollars will sell them, and that could trigger the end of the world banking and financial system of this era. This is only one bomb, but there are many other "credit rising bombs" ready to explode, reacting then a nuclear financial bomb.

This breakdown will cause political, social, and cultural changes as well. It will set the stage for an epic transformation. It will destroy the power and wealth of the ruling elite, since their main assets were Treasury securities, thus setting the stage for root change in America.

Coupled with bankruptcy will be the end of the industrial era. We are witness to an epic transformation of man. Lewis Mumford wrote in *The Transformation of Man* that there have been five major transformations in mankind in the last 10,000 years, the last major one being the emergence of the industrial society. Now that, too, is ending, like all good things.

NATIONAL DEFAULTS—AGES OLD

Although the American federal government is on the road to its own one-of-a-kind debt repudiation, this unfortunate process is as old as economic history, going back to the earliest times. There was the crisis in Germany, after World War I, that brought them hyperinflation and ruin and Adolph Hitler. This is but one recent example.

But a crisis with an eery historical parallel to our own times was the severe financial crisis in France that occurred in 1788-1798. [5]

Every history of the French Revolution discussed the important role of the financial crisis of 1788-1789 played at the end of the ancient regime. Louis XVI convened the Estates General to deal with their catastrophic fiscal crisis. It emerged because of a serious effort to effect controlled structural change by the old order by borrowing instead of raising taxes. And, it was also a veiled attempt to preserve the ruling elite and their power. But their clumsy strategy at that time failed abysmally because the established regimes transferred part of their political legitimacy to articulate dissidents representing the (at first) peaceful popular protest movements.

The dissident leaders agreed to a power-sharing arrangement that was quickly undermined by the bungling and subterfuges of the old order, and by public outrage at the privileges and excesses of the much-resented power elite. Under those circumstances, the dissident leaders and institutions took it upon themselves the right to speak with the authority of the entire nation. In this historic moment, the fall of the tangible symbol of oppression marked the political collapse of the hated elite. And in 1789 the fall of the Bastille was the symbol. It embodied the force of political coercion and the denial of basic human rights that had characterized the old order.

To replace the latter system, dissident leaders promulgated legal documents abolishing undeserved privileges, defining the rights of the individual with respect to the state, and establishing a governmental structure responsive to the idea of true popular sovereignty.

By August 1789, the political revolution in France had been achieved. What remained was to rectify the social and economic injustices that ran contrary to the evolutionary ideals of liberty and equality.

The French regime rested on certain basic elements like our system does today: they collected taxes through a large number of agencies instead of an Internal Revenue Service like we have. Whenever they had a deficit, they issued a variety of debt instruments to raise funds, just exactly as we have done. The continually spent more than they received in taxes, and financed their deficits by borrowing more, just as we have done.

The decline in France was gradual, as ours has been. Every effort with new financial reforms to reestablish the government's credit failed. And the large and rich private creditors of the government were furious, as ours are now.

The more things change, the more they are the same.

The chaotic financial difficulties of Uncle Sam have a startling parallel with those experienced by the French monarchy in 1789, before Napoleon.

In France, the government debt, already huge when Louis XVI came to power, tripled between 1774 and 1789, and half of this increase came from French participation in the American War of Independence. In 1789, the debt stood at 4,500,000,000 livres. The budget for 1788, the only one computed for the Old Regime, made alarming reading:

French Budget 1788

Estimated expenses	(in livres)
For debt service	318,000,000
For the court	35,000,000
For other purposes	276,000,000
Total	629,000,000
Estimated revenues	503,000,000
Estimated deficit	126,000,000

Source: *History of Civilization*

"Especially disturbing was the very high proportion of revenues consumed by interest payments on debts already contracted."[6]

This has a familiar ring to it. The King was warned of the danger back then, but ignored it and continued to raise new loans. Sounds familiar.

From 1783 to 1786, 653,000,000 livres was raised in new loans. And in 1786 the bankers refused to make new advances. The French government was then caught between the forces of the third estate's demands for tax relief and the refusal by other estates to give up their tax exemptions.

After a series of mounting troubles over time, the financial disruptions in France were overrun by Napoleon coming to power in 1789.

The French government borrowed from the banking system until they could do this no more.

They tried new forms of taxes, and these also failed.

Then, in 1788, an economic depression emerged, like ours now, causing government expenditures to rise and revenues to decline—just as ours have done.

In this long process, creditors were assured over and over again that the nation's debts were sacred obligations.

Still, tax increases were impossible, and bankruptcy was

politically dangerous. At this juncture, they shifted from deficit financing to fiat money financing, like the Latin nations have done since 1982. And this paper money policy also failed.

Those in power did not understand this train of events. But the revolutionaries back then did.

Finally in 1797, default on French national debts came when all remedies had been exhausted. It had taken nine years.

MEASURING AMERICAN GOVERNMENT CREDITWORTHINESS

One historical measure of national creditworthiness was how long a time the government will be allowed to borrow money. In other words, the longer the period the the public would lend its money to the government, the higher the government's creditworthiness. Thus, if the public is willing to lend for thirty years, then the government's credit was prime, and in the 1930s, with all of its travails, the American Government was perfectly creditworthy. At the turn of the century, some American Treasury Bonds had maturities of one hundred years. By 1990 the average maturity of all U.S. debts had shrunk to 4-1/2 years—and the slide was accelerating.

AMERICAN SITUATION IS GRIMMER THAN FRANCE'S WAS

The breakdown in our federal government's finances comes at a far worse time for the entire nation that the debt problems in France were for them. In France, there were no internal debts like ours: our consumers, corporations and cities and states themselves are all buried under enormous debt loads. Thus national bankruptcy for Americans means the entire domestic structure crashing down on our heads and not just the federal government's. This event destroys all, as the credit-dollar becomes worthless in the federal default process. So, every institution in America is either insolvent, bankrupt or nearly there.

Where will the new credits come from now to get America going again? That is the topic of a later chapter: The time has come for debt-free money.

THE FRENCH FISCAL HISTORY

Long-Term Debt is now Short-Term Debt.

Times have changed. By 1990 the average maturity of U.S. Treasury Debt had contracted to 4-1/2 years—and the time span that the funds were being loaned for continued to shrink. This means debt maturities will shrink from 4-1/2 years to the 90-day maturity of a Treasury Bill: the debt roll over sums are vast— $700 billion a year, for example. The Bond market will collapse into the Bill market because the public will not lend for a long time to a risky debtor.

LIKE BRAZIL?

By the fall of 1989, Brazil's financial economy was developing into a full-fledged disaster. The domestic public debt of $50 billion had a maturity of *less than one day,* according to Dr. Rudiger Dornbusch, in *World Link Magazine*.[7]

Could Brazil continue to roll over this enormous debt day after day? Dr. Rudiger's answer was, "No" "When the country's domestic debt bubble bursts, the country's entire financial system will blow up."

Postscript: That may have happened by the time you read this. The consequences of that failure, coupled with Argentina, Mexico and others defaulting, would virtually demolish the world monetary and banking systems, presenting Financial Doomsday in still another dress.

FIRST PUBLIC NOTICE OF FEDERAL DEBT PROBLEMS

Although the federal debts and deficits had been relentlessly growing, there was almost no media or official recognition of the giant-size of the entire problem. Also, the public was being deceived: gigantic as federal deficits became, they did not reveal the entire story because federal budget deficits and federal debt growth are not the same. For example, in 1988 the federal budget deficit was approximately $155 billion while the federal debt increase was nearly $255 billion. Much of the government debt was being financed "off-budget," i.e., hidden from public scrutiny by borrowing money, but by doing it off the formal, and publicized, deficit data.

THE GENERAL ACCOUNTING OFFICE ASSESSES THE PROBLEM

By the late fall of 1989, the enormity of the problem came into public focus with the revelations of a study by the General Accounting Office. In this report, they revealed that the federal government's habit of creating popular loan programs and credit plans as cheap alternatives to outright government spending had mushroomed into a potentially devastating financial problem. It amounted to five trillion dollars in assorted obligations, varying from direct student loans to insurance of bank deposits and mortgages. Note the findings in this table:

BUILDING CREDIT

Federal credit obligations, in billions of dollars

	1965	1988	Increase
Direct loans	$33	$222	573%
Loan guarantees	91	550	504
Loans to government-sponsored enterprises	15	666	4,340
Insurance commitments	299	3,617	1,110
Total	$438	$5,055	1,054%

SOURCE: General Accounting Office

Source: *Los Angeles Times*, November 23, 1989

According to the study, the total of the federal programs equalled the annual gross national product and amounted to roughly $20,000 for every man, woman and child in the country. It had grown ten times since 1965.

Taxpayers, it was estimated, would face an eventual bill estimated by the General Accounting Office of $139 billion to make good on federal insurance of deposits on hundreds of failed S&Ls. But, *Barron's* newspaper estimated the loss at more like $964 billion.[8]

Not only that, mounting losses on other programs posed the threat of new drains on the U.S. Treasury. Because the General Accounting Office estimated the government's risk to be heightened because loan defaults were rising steadily, and new government guarantees were becoming more risky, and the solvency of many insurance programs was questionable.

The size of the problem was so enormous that the Accounting Agency said that "estimating the size of the problem remains impossible. Even the magnitude of losses already suffered by the government cannot be determined because of inadequate accounting and monitoring procedures in the programs."

Illustrating this problem, the Federal Housing Administration (HUD) had estimated its losses of 1988 at $858 million for four mortgage insurance programs, but in September 1989 the General Accounting Office found the losses were actually much worse—$4.2 billion for the same period, six times larger. But these problems surfaced in the programs: federal crop insurance, student loans, veterans' home-loan insurance funds, and pension benefit guarantees for 76 million workers, etc.

CHICKENS COME HOME TO ROOST

Although the public seemed removed and disinterested in federal government finances, the bills were falling due in Washington the same as they always fall due for anyone in debt when debts become too burdensome. The reality was that America was bankrupt, and the fiction of solvency was gradually melting away. At every level in America—consumers, corporations, cities and states, and now the federal government—we had squandered ourselves into the position where the total deflation of debt was imperative and unavoidable. The disease factor of debt which kept the "capitalist system" continuing was becoming terminal. I refer to the "capitalist system" which is what most human beings adore, but it is neither essentially capitalistic nor very much of a system. It seemed to be rather queer, adaptable and usually workable improvisation based upon the hope of taking profit through the use of debt at compound interest. Capital is one thing; capital-at-interest is not quite the same thing.

THE INTEREST BURDEN

The General Accounting Office data, while complete, failed to deal with compound interest which accompanies virtually all debt. There is a Rule of 72, which gives a measure of how long it takes interest to double: 8% goes into 72 nine times, so in nine years, $1,000 becomes $2,000. Now, with $5 trillion of debt at 8%, this debt would become $10 trillion by the turn of the century. Beyond that, $5 trillion in debt requires, at 8%, $400 billion a year simply to pay ongoing interest on it, enlarging the debt to $5.4 trillion the next year, and so on.

Real interest rates
Short-term rates deflated by consumer prices

United States

Britain

• Latest

Household debt
as % of disposable income

United States

Britain

1975 77 79 81 83 85 87 88

Sources: CSO; Federal Reserve; Bank of England; IMF; Phillips & Drew

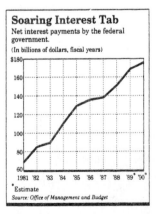

Soaring Interest Tab
Net interest payments by the federal government.
(In billions of dollars, fiscal years)

1981 '82 '83 '84 '85 '86 '87 '88 '89 '90

*Estimate

Source: Office of Management and Budget

It does not take an advanced degree in mathematics to see that by late 1989 it was rapidly becoming impossible to generate the credit funds, to borrow more, at any level, to repay the rapidly growing debt.

It is now only a question of time until the federal government would have to take steps to delay this event. They could do this by transferring their enormous short-term debts into long-term debts, i.e., make a 90-Day Treasury Bill's principal due in 30 years, not 90 days, and paying interest when and *if* they could. It has happened in other countries before now, so it would be a history lesson coming back to haunt us.

But, when this event emerges full blown, it will bring a dramatic and radical redistribution of income. This is because large sums of money are invested in government obligations by banks, by individuals, by corporations, etc. This action would leave them impoverished.

But those who own Treasury Debts are not stupid. They will muster all the forces they can to forestall this event. But, alas, it will be in vain. The debts will be settled by default—the historic solution since debts are always paid by either the creditor or the debtor. Our time is no different, but it is for us, really, since it is happening in "our time."

DEEPER INTO THE DEBT HOLE

It is interesting that despite the enormous growth in debt, the problem was virtually ignored by politicians and their economists. Debt was perceived to be "not a problem." Why? They argued that with the low interest rates of 2 and 3% prevailing years ago, reasonable high economic growth would prevent the American national debt from becoming too burdensome. This was all that economists had to know about debt for most of the post-war period in America, since real interest rates were much

beneath growth rates—in both developed and developing countries—in the 1950s, 1960s, and 1970s. But, the game changed in
1981: real dollar interest rates rose abruptly to levels far above
sustainable economic growth rates. This rapid rise in real rates
increased the risk that fiscal reflation would lead to an explosive
increase in public debt which, of course, it did. Among other
things, it proved the futility of the supply-side economist theory
that emerged during that time.

It is a historical truism that when real interest rates are above
the growth rate of incomes, borrowers will tumble into a debt
hole. This is because the accumulation of compound interest
charged makes debt growth unsustainable.

In the developing countries, it became clear that their financial difficulties were another example of this debt hole. The
relationship between the interest rates on the debt they owed
outside their country and the growth rates of their exports was
critical to their long-run solvency. It is the same as the solvency
problem that arose between the interest rates on domestic debt
and the growth rate of national income in America.

Explosive debt in all its forms is not new in economic
history. Evidence of legally enforceable debt contracts in ancient
Egypt and Assyria have been found by archaeologists. A banking
system, which is our modern method of registering and settling
debts, operated in an advanced form 2,000 years ago in Ptole-
maic Egypt.

Beyond that, many economists argued that the growth of
financial systems and the accompanying increase in debt contributed to material progress, so debt was good. In the past, debt
growth may have been benign, but now it is not. This is because
we must make a sharp distinction between increases in debt
which are sustainable and *increases in debt which are
unsustainable*. Increases in debt are unsustainable when the
borrower, sooner or later, finds himself unable to repay the

lender in full. The most glaring example of this was during the Great Depression. Since a nation can owe nothing to itself, it is an absurd idea that banks and factories close down because the citizens cannot pay their debts to each other. But that is precisely what happened.

Back in the 1930s, 9,000 banks shut down, and industrial production fell by 40% while unemployment rose to 25%. Back then, the sudden and massive rise in the ratio of debt to total income was perhaps the central cause of that debacle. As companies and individuals found themselves unable to service this debt, they could not repay their bank loans. Banks shut down, causing a general credit contraction which made the slump in demand worse—a domino effect.

Debt to income ratios are sustainable if borrowers and lenders are well informed about their respective circumstances and borrowers are paying both principal and interest on their debts. If, as in American past history, a certain ratio has been established between debt and income and debt is growing in line with rising income, then there is no need to be worried about too much debt. So, we did not worry. But the debt income ratio cannot increase indefinitely. Most lenders want to have assurance that their loans are backed not merely by the personal guarantee of the borrower, but by solid physical things of recognized value. They want debt to be secured against tangible assets. As debts increase, collateral diminishes, so as new debt is added without adequate collateral, then the debt problem worsens gravely.

America's debt to income ratio can rise over time, but only up to the point at which debt is finite proportion of the value of tangible assets and at that at the very outside by 1 to 2% per year in the long run. If either or both of these conditions are broken, the growth in debt is unsustainable.

Note this chart:

The USA's/income ratio starts to rise just as real interest rates move ahead of the growth rate, 1971-1985.

i. Real dollar interest rates compared with the growth rate

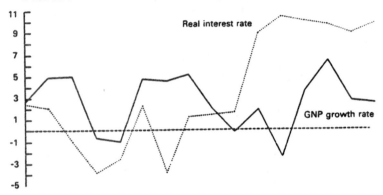

Data Source: Economic Report of the President, 1983. Tables B-61 and B-68.

Since 1981, the debt to income ratio has been rising over 5% a year, far above the 1 or 2% a year that is sustainable. So, the present growth in debt is unsustainable, as are present debt loads. Therefore, it is a mathematical certainty that much of the excess debt loads in America are bound to implode. And we are already seeing that event happening in rising bankruptcies, foreclosures, defaults, etc.

ANOTHER SHOE TO DROP

It was estimated in late 1989 that 17 countries in the world owed the world banking system between $523 billion and $1.2 trillion.[9] The banks alone were owed $280 billion. The final outcome of this debt cloud can only be global disaster. There is a good reason for this: for openers, no Latin nation has repaid a debt since 1800, so why will they pay now? Beyond that, they simply do not have the resources to pay back.

When this event unfolds during the 1990s, it is safe to

predict, as some have, that this would amount to the breakdown of Western Civilization and the disintegration of the international financial system. Why?

If the banks cannot retrieve the vast capital sums they have loaned, they will not have the resources to repay their depositors globally the sums that will be demanded. Billions of credit dollars were created out of thin air and will go back into thin air, leaving a world destitute, a world without credit dollars. This is no exaggeration. All the while this has been developing, it has been the accepted wisdom that governments would intervene and create the missing credit dollars, but most governments were themselves financially strapped with too much debt, and could only get the funds they needed by borrowing more, worsening the problem instead of solving it. A total Catch 22 was in the making.

PUBLIC DEBT DILEMMA

In 1777 and 1778, Congress issued too much paper money to finance the Revolutionary War. This paper money was known as "Continentals," which quickly lost their value and brought on a violent inflation. In March 1880, Congress redeemed them at one-fortieth of their face value—the first American repudiation. From then on, fiscal conservatism became the American golden rule.

After Alexander Hamilton resigned as the first Secretary of the Treasury, he prepared a Valedictory Report in which he outlined the cardinal principles on which the nation's finances should be guided and run. He warned that, "The progressive accumulation of debt must ultimately endanger all Government," and recommended a sinking fund be established to extinguish debts over a thirty-year period. In 1895, a historian wrote about the Sinking Fund Act of 1799, enacted to accomplish Hamilton's ideas:

"First of all it established distinctive revenues for the payment of interest on the public debt as well as for the reimbursing of the principal within a determinate period. Second, it directed imperatively their application to the debt alone; third, it pledged the faith of the Government that the appointed revenues should continue to be levied and collected and appropriated to these objects until the whole debt should be redeemed." [10]

This pattern of beliefs saw the national debt of $127 million in 1815, and of $2.7 billion in 1865, reduced to $1 billion by 1893. Those ideas were the mainstream orthodoxy until the 1930s.

Debt is a destabilizing force and, given time, stands a society on its head financially and economically. Debt is also the overwhelming, and the number one cause of all depressions in our form of economic system. And, yet, we have abandoned our resistance to debt formation. Why?

Many believe it was the economic ideas of Lord Keynes who proposed deficit financing in the 1930s. But, in the 1930s the ideas for government borrowing and spending were not those of Keynes, but those of Marriner Eccles who had never read Keynes. [11] He was Chairman of the Federal Reserve Board and on that Board for seventeen years. Early on, the notion of America going into debt was resisted, especially in the 1930s by Lewis Douglas, then Director of the Budget who declared that this debt path would ultimately see "The end of Western Civilization."

It has taken almost sixty years for us to realize the wisdom of that prophecy.

But from the 1930s until now, debt was perceived to be "good." Generations of economists taught that idea, and politicians put debt into motion. Why? Well, two things are true: 1) The public hates any form of taxation, and 2) flooding a society artificially with credit dollars, "the borrow and spend notion," helps to promote prosperity, albeit an artificial one. For awhile it provides the illusion of good times, but all parties end, and now we are witness to the supreme folly of living on debt—most especially abusing public debt.

By the time of the Reagan Administration, flawed economic ideas had reached another plateau—one of the platforms of the spurious supply-side economists of those days was the belief that by lowering tax rates, this would cause the American economy to generate more tax revenues. It capped the breakdown of historic and traditional views on sound government finance had replaced them with a welter of confusing, conflicting, and absurd doctrines. And now we face the savage penalties.

The abandoning of old-time fiscal religion and conservative ideas of debt led to the present deterioration in public morals. And also to a change in public attitudes towards debt.

This has led us to where we are now: unsustainable debts because interest rates are growing faster than economic growth, thus insuring public debts will only be repudiated, sooner or later. There is no other escape. This phenomenon will be accelerated as hard times raises debts higher and interest rates also, thus foreshortening the moment of truth.

IN DEBT WE TRUST

This is how the *Wall Street Journal* described the United States' debt obligations to foreigners. "For the first time since 1914 the U.S. in 1985 owed more to other nations than they owed to it," they wrote. But owing debts to foreigners is one problem. Having large and unsustainable domestic debts is another and perhaps more frightening problem.

How did America go from a nation that was fiscally conservative to a nation where domestic debts grew larger and more dangerous than those in the so-called Banana Republics?

As I note in Chapter 2, one compelling reason was to expand social benefits by borrowing funds and do this without raising taxes. The tax relief insured that there would be a redistribution of income from the rich to the middle class and poor, so the borrowing vehicle was selected since it provided the rich with a low risk, high return for their own surplus funds, and did not redistribute income away from them. But there is more.

Also, for fifteen years after World War II, American public finances were managed with extraordinary care. After getting over the spending binge of that war, America was running a surplus as soon as 1947 of $14 billion. From 1947 to 1960 there were seven surpluses and seven deficit years. The cumulative sum of these surpluses and deficits was a minus figure of $0.8 billion.

During this period it is interesting to note that nominal GNP grew by an average of 7.1 percent a year while the yield on the yield on ten-year U.S. Treasury debts was about 2-1/2 percent. This meant that the compounded growth of GNP being larger than that of compounded debt growth insured that funds would be available to repay the debts.[12]

But then things changed—gradually responsible federal finance turned into their irresponsible finance we have had since then. The war in Southeast Asia was a contributor, but also there was an even more deep reason: there emerged a generation of economists who believe, and taught, that debts were of no concern—we owed the debt to ourselves, so it was going from one pocket to another, and so on. Most of these mathematically trained economists, for a very curious reason, never commented on, or seemed notice, the power of compound interest. They, of all people, should have focused on that power especially with their mathematical mentalities.

But these ideas are now proving to be fatal. It is the self-feeding phenomena of compound interest that has upset the public debt applecart and brought us to our unstable and dangerous position today.

People who get mixed up with loan sharks invariably are faced with bigger and bigger interest payments, and rarely are they able to pay off their debts. Uncle Sam is not exactly in hock to the mob, but the government has got itself into such a mix.

Huge deficits, combined with record interest rates, have made the cost of servicing the U.S. debt the fastest-rising component of government spending. Interest payments climbed from $89 billion in 1983 to $265 billion in 1989, actually over $200 billion, but some of the costs were hidden by using funds borrowed from Social Security surpluses. For a long time interest rates have been rising faster than the Gross National Product—in 1980 the national debt was $930 billion, or about 35% of the GNP. By 1983 it had surged to $1.4 trillion, or 43% of GNP. And by the end of 1988 the national debt was over $2.5 trillion, close to half of the GNP. It was becoming a case of where the miracle of compound interest was working *against* the government. More and more resources now went just to debt payment and debt service.

The burden of federal debt service on taxpayers has doubled in just 10 years: in 1989, 50 cents of every dollar paid by individual taxpayers was used to service (pay interest) on federal debts. In 1979, only 28 cents of individual tax receipts was required. At this rate, by the year 2000, over 100% of every dollar paid in taxes by individuals will be needed to pay interest. [13]

Cutting federal deficits became an exercise in futility: interest payments were an uncontrollable expense because if they were not paid, then the government faced default. In 1978 this item accounted for 7.9% of total government spending. By 1988 it accounted for 11.6% according to the Government Budget Office.[14] As interest rates rise, this cost rises, of course.

And, as time went on, more and more income was shifted to foreign debt owners. And it also represented a shift in income to investors of government securities since those in higher brackets own most of them and this takes income from the lower classes and gives it to them.

Debt does not grow each year by the addition of interest charges, but by the addition of interest charges less the tax on them. So we should look to the post-tax rate instead of the pre-tax rate, but the result is always the same: the public debt continues to rise explosively as this post-tax rate on debt exceeds the growth rate of GNP. This is unsustainable.

The variables are now out of control: interest rates rising, growth of GNP falling and probably some rising tax rates on debt interest receipts. With the economy contracting as it was in 1989 and 1990, credit was becoming tighter, meaning higher rates of interest, thus worsening this variable. A slowing down of the economy meant less GNP growth, of course—so we have reached the worst of both worlds, rising interest rates with a lower GNP, making the whole problem still more unsustainable and dangerous for all of us.

Now we have reached a threatening dilemma: hard times are on us. More federal funds are needed to fund social welfare and unemployment. The funds can only come from more borrowing at high rates of interest. With deficits of $400 billion and more in the 1990s and interest rates close to 8%, the government's finances are on a path to debt repudiation.

Uncle Sam cannot continue to borrow forever any more than any other debtor can. Some day soon, as debt growth accelerates, buyers of debt will wonder if the debts will ever be serviced, much less paid, and then start to slow down their purchases. If the government attempts to force the debts on the buyers, this is also a threat to the credit of the government. A total Catch 22 has been made.

CONTINUING THE PUBLIC DEBT ILLUSION

The matter of managing public debt became, by the 1990s, a financial game where the participants devoted their skills to hiding spending by keeping items "off-budget," that is, spending but keeping it from the public eye.

For example, in 1989 $100 million was spent for a Judicial Office Building. But instead of having the Treasury borrow the money (on budget financing), it was decided to use off-budget financing.

This meant that the money to pay for the building would be raised by using the federal government's credit indirectly. Instead of having Congress appropriate the money and the Treasury borrow the money on the federal government's credit. This off-budget, slight-of-hand would keep the building's cost out of the federal budget until 1944. But, what about the fact that this would make federal spending from 1994 to 2024 larger than it would otherwise be? They would worry about that when they got there.

The funds to build the building were thus raised on Wall Street by them selling esoteric paper called Federal Judiciary Office Building Serial Zero Coupon Certificates of Participation. They issued 62 of these each with a face value of $8,615,000 and they start falling due every six months starting in August 1994. The money to pay for these securities as they fall due will come from the lease payments that the federal government will pay the owner of the building, a Boston Properties partnership.

What did this trick of paper shuffling cost the public? The Wall Street firms that marketed them got fees of close to $2 million. Then there was the interest on them of 8.55% a year, higher than Treasury interest rates. The added interest costs amounted to $10 million over the 35-year life of the JOB securities.

But this example was only one of many, many ways used to hide borrowing and deflect the attention of the public. The largest during this period was the rescue plan for the savings and loan industry, the Resolution Trust Corporation which initially sold $4.52 billion of 30-year bonds, the interest cost of going off-budget was 0.28% of 1% a year, which adds up to $380 million extra.

Now the funny money games were ending and the piper was to be paid.

THE GROWTH OF PUBLIC DEBT

Since the Great Depression, the federal government has been running on more and more debt, as this table shows. The enormous rise since 1981 was pretty generally ignored by the public because they, too, were busy incurring large debts and did not think the whole debt process to be harmful to them or to America. It was believed to be okay, and beyond that economic experts told them that debts were "good," that we owed the money to ourselves, that it was an insignificant part of our GNP, and so on.

PUBLIC DEBT OF AND INTEREST PAID BY THE FEDERAL GOVERNMENT, 1940–87

	PUBLIC DEBT			INTEREST PAID	
Year	Total[1] (bils. of dollars)	Average annual percent change[2]	Per capita[3] (dollars)	Total (bils. of dollars)	Percent of federal outlays[4]
1940	$ 43.0	8.4%	$ 325	$ 1.0	10.5%
1945	256.7	43.0	1,849	3.8	4.1
1950	256.1	-0.1	1,698	5.7	13.4
1955	272.8	1.3	1,651	6.4	9.4
1960	284.1	0.9	1,572	9.2	10.0
1965	313.8	2.0	1,613	11.3	9.6
1970	370.1	3.3	1,814	19.3	9.9
1971	397.3	7.4	1,921	21.0	10.0
1972	426.4	7.3	2,037	21.8	9.4
1973	457.3	7.2	2,164	24.2	9.8
1974	474.2	3.7	2,223	29.3	10.9
1975	533.2	12.4	2,475	32.7	9.8
1976	620.4	16.4	2,852	37.1	10.0
1977	698.8	10.1	3,170	41.9	10.2
1978	771.5	10.4	3,463	48.7	10.6
1979	826.5	7.1	3,669	59.8	11.9
1980	907.7	9.8	3,985	74.9	12.7
1981	997.9	9.9	4,338	95.6	14.1
1982	1,142.0	14.4	4,913	117.4	15.7
1983	1,377.2	20.6	5,870	128.8	15.9
1984	1,572.3	14.2	6,640	153.8	18.1
1985	1,823.1	16.0	7,616	178.9	18.9
1986	2,125.3	16.6	8,793	187.1	18.9
1987	2,350.3	10.6	9,630	195.4	19.5

	Debt owed by domestic non-financial sectors ($b)	GNP at annual rates	Debt/income ratio
1952	461.1	364.0	1.267
1962	822.7	582.8	1.412
1972	1,725.9	1,263.5	1.366
1982	4,679.1	3,212.5	1.457
1983	5,230.6	3,545.8	1.475
1984	5,985.4	3,851.8	1.554
1985	6,851.0	4,104.4	1.669
1986	7,678.9	4,288.1	1.791

Debt figures refer to end-year, GNP figures to fourth quarter, seasonally adjusted.

Sources: U.S. Department of Commerce, Bureau of Economic Analysis, and *National Income and Product Accounts of the United States*, table 1.1.

But from the beginning of economic time, public debts have been generally ruinous, as we are finding out (or will soon discover). A line from the Merchant of Venice, Act II, Scene 2, describes this as "The seeming truth which cunning times put on. To entrap the wisest." It has done that to all of us.

PUBLIC DEBT HISTORY: U.S. AND BRITAIN

Early economists viewed public borrowing as evil, thinking that a nation no less than an individual should earn its money before spending it. But this old idea has been jerked out of our modern banker-economy. We have been told that the manipulation of public credit "within certain bounds" is a blessing; that it may even account for the great advance in human comfort and happiness in the past two hundred years. It is pointed out over and over that at every stage of growth of public debt, people fearing this have predicted ruin and bankruptcy have been at hand. The increase in wealth coincident with the increase in public debt has been greeted with great joy in America.

Economists tell us how wonderful public debt is: it makes men work harder, it will develop new sources of wealth, Treasury paper debts supply a new kind of money upon which business can be based, business thrives on debt, and so on—the blessings that flow from the creation of public debts.

But those who cherish public borrowing draw their conclusions from just two nations—England and America—the two nations that have progressed the most in the past two centuries when the great industrial and trading age arrived. But the public debt did cost England the American colonies. England wanted to pass on debt service to the colonials who refused it.

The case of the United States is a marvel in development which has no parallel in world history. Nowhere was there such a body of land to be exploited, and never anywhere an immigration with such genius for tapping those hidden riches. So rapid was the production of wealth that America could, during most of its life, have carried a much larger debt than it did had it been necessary.

And neither Great Britain or the United States has ever defaulted on its public debts, though other nations cruise on an ocean of defaults, repudiations, inflations, refundings, forced settlements, swindles, and political robbery that sickens the mind.

In a historical study of debt in France and England, these conclusions can be drawn:

1) Those who say that debt burden is nothing at all have a totally false view. The ability to repay debt depends on circumstances which those who incur it cannot control or know ahead of time.

2) Incurring debt is a policy of weakness, not strength.

3) A nation can thrive in spite of, but not because of, the load of public debt.

THE TREASURY

The opposite of public debt is the public treasury. If America's finances were in good shape, the Treasury Department should store the reserves of the society. But it has been transformed into repository of debt memoranda where the actual money flowing in and out is encumbered in advance of its collection from the public in the form of taxes, and where the so-called "balanced budget" is triumph of skill.

But economists and politicians tell us that we should possess public debt instead of public reserves. The greater danger in having public debt is that in the minds of the public, they are forever confused as to what their public debt really is. In fact, they are so confused that they most often think of public debt as public "reserves." The reality is that virtually every modern state is penniless, and worse. Any balances they have await dispersal to dependents and creditors while its tax-gathering agencies are feverishly active. It is also forgotten that the money of the government is always a liability, always a debt. It would be more prudent then to all the Secretary of the Treasury the Secretary of Debt.

Public debt is a device intended to beguile the taxpayer into thinking that he is getting something for nothing.

Any methods of incurring debt leaves the society with the same economic results. The debt must always be serviced and finally paid back, or defaulted on. As John Ruskin wrote, "Public indebtedness always ends by taking the peasant by the throat, and he must pay for only he can pay."

THE MATTER OF DEBT SERVICE

In the late 1980s, the average rate of interest in America was about 8%. A mathematical friend of mine calculated that if the American government stopped borrowing in 1989, and if interest rates did not rise above 8%, then in the future interest payments would be 100% of all federal spending by the year 2020. If the government continued to borrow, which it has been doing, then that level would be reached between 1994 and 1998. Think about this: all of the income generated would be siphoned off just on the public debt. This would allow very little, if anything, to repay $9 trillion in private debts. Thus the society will deflate and credit will implode on a vast scale.

Astonishingly, however, by 1990 no one seemed to pay much attention to this dangerous and growing threat.

It only makes sense that if interest is growing at 8%, compounded, then the means to repay it must also grow at 8%. But that was not happening in America in the 1980s—GNP growth never attained that level. So, the new debt added to the old debt was simply breeding more bad debt. And at 8% interest compounding, the total debt was doubling in just nine years.

This same phenomena was true of all debt: if as a consumer you could not earn more than the interest rate on your debts, then you could not gain on them. You were always behind. It was no small wonder, then, that consumers enmired in debt were truly trapped.

THE IDEA OF A SINKING FUND

All through history in many societies, the public debt was either intended to ultimately be paid off or it was not. If there is any notion in mind that it be paid off, then the promises of a definite maturity should be accompanied by a sinking fund to insure the debt would be retired. If it was not intended that it be repaid, it then takes the form of a perpetual loan upon which no one is likely to propose any payment other than that necessary to pay the interest charges. So politicians have always found debt like a cork—easier to float than to sink. It can be said of the Reagan Administration that it was tempting to make him a great figure by not burdening the people with taxes, and concurrently abusing the contracting of debt. This created an aura of good feeling and good times which was really a false prosperity as we now know.

A public debt, like America's, which is in the form of bonds and notes and bills is a handy medium for the investment of surpluses. They also form an additional basis of credit, and a circulating medium, until the fatal time when they may flow back into the bank portfolios in such large numbers that they convert banks into pipelines for government debt. But for the rich they are the best of all investments since the paper debts provide a usury income with the least possible risk.

The assumption that American debt can constantly grow implies a belief in constant economic growth of wealth to infinity. In other words, in so far as we know nature, this concept is based on a transparent fallacy. As Napoleon wrote, "National debt is immoral and destructive, silently undermining the basis of the state; it delivers the present generation to the execration of posterity."

A curious fact about public debt is that no matter how honorable was the intent of the borrowing government at the time the loan is made, the time of the loan used to be so long that it was a certainty that the politicians who originally contracted the debt would no longer be in power. The majority of governments probably neither intend to swindle nor appear as bad risks. And most of the public borrowing is in this category.

NATIONAL BANKRUPTCY HISTORY

It is well then to now remind us of the more famous bankruptcies of the nineteenth century, previous to World War I: Spain in 1820, 1831, 1834, 1851, 1867, 1872; Greece in 1836 and 1893; Denmark in 1812, 1813; Prussia in 1807 and 1813; Austria in 1802, 1805, 1806, 1811, 1816, 1868; Holland in 1814; Portugal in 1830, 1853, 1892; Russia in 1839; Turkey in 1875 and 1881. During much of this period, most of the debts of Latin American nations could not be quoted. And for more than half a century, the American States, sometimes a dozen of them at one time, were on the black list of the continental lenders.

These bankruptcies do not imply the creditors were completely wiped out. Quite the contrary, failed governments all made efforts to shore up their finances so they could return to the money markets as fast as possible.

After World War I, public debts around the world resembled bedlam. Now in 1990, the situation is much the same: the Latin Nations, African nations, nations in the Far East, are solvent by rhetorical courtesy, or the difficulty by the world bankers in deciding what constitutes bankruptcy in this unique era.

Public debts really represented deferred taxation, but nonetheless in America they have grown like Topsy because of the dexterity of our politicians and the gullibility of the citizen taxpayer who has been led to believe that:

1) Debts will be easier to pay next year than this year.
2) He is getting something for nothing.

These illusions provide fertile soil for politicians and their economists who tell the public that public debt is really the credit base, and a push for production, and that it is really just transferring wealth from the right hand to the left. These efforts will always result in the public debt reaching the vast proportions it has now in America—a pyramid so monumental that the American public should prepare for the shock to come. But no one does—so deep is the faith. Alas.

The economist/philosopher David Hume wrote about this long ago, "The nation being heartily sick of its debts and cruelly oppressed by them, some daring projector may arise with visionary schemes for their discharge." In the past, the "daring projector" was like John Law in France who peddled in France the deadly notion of perpetual prosperity. In modern times, the projector is a demagogue or a deluded zealot who will practice on the simplicity of the public in the hard times that now emerge.

Is a "daring projector" in our future? Probably.

In economic history, the identical subterfuges, ingenuities, and incantations recur with precise regularity. "He who is ignorant of history remains always a child," said Cicero. But he might have better said, "He who is incapable of making prudent inference form history."

But the true statesman sees the background motives clearly. Edmund Burke wrote, "Real money can hardly ever multiply too much in any country because it will always as it increases be a certain sign of the increase of trade, of which it is the measure, and consequently of the soundness and vigor of the whole body. But when paper money is used, which is not real money, and it increases without any increase in trade, often when trade is declining, it does not measure trade, but the necessity of the government. Alexander Hamilton wrote, "In great and trying times there is almost a moral certainty of paper money becoming mischievous." But, despite the stark lessons of paper money history, we will hear the clarion call for more paper money to get us out of our bad times. All through history the failed nostrums repeat, and they tug on the mind of the public who deal mainly in paper money and understand little of credit and debt money.

Perhaps the most brilliant democrats that ever lived were the Athenians. But, with all their blunders, the Athenians, as free men, never indulged in the final madness of debasing their currency. By contrast, they rose in trade by means of establishing good credit, and by safeguarding the honor of their coins.

Politicians are astute in converting the phenomena of public debt to their own advantage. Many American political parties have come to power upon a platform of economy—but never twice. We often here that a politician is equipped with a "mandate" from his constituents toward economy in government. What this really means is that he is directed by his electors to urge other politicians to spend less, so that his district can spend more. Each votes as much as possible. In politics, the word economy refers to something somebody else has done or is to be required to do or not to do.

The average man who has had experience with some of the joys of borrowing and the pains of repayment might balk at the idea of the government frivolously borrowing if he thought of the state as being financially comparable to himself. But he does not. His ideas of the finances of government are vague enough, but, worse, he thinks of the state as possessing some supramundane power which enables it to defy or glide over natural laws. He cannot imagine, for example, a government in bankruptcy, though he can easily see himself, or his friends, in that position.

Normally, politicians fulfill their promises by voting great expenditures of money. To vote taxes that equal that spending would be unpopular, so recourse is had to borrowing, and the creation of funded debt. With money in his hand, the politician can secure his position by benefiting dependents, steering contracts, stimulating employment, and translating money into material things that respond to real need. He "puts money into circulation," it is said.

The flaw in this is that the politicians' predecessors have done the same thing, and there is a large debt load from the past already being carried. So, in modern times the management of debt grows in importance, but the problem of refunding debts and trying to keep spending up would cause sleepless nights to a businessman only whets the adroitness of the politicians.

Government debt creates, then, exactly that sort of shadowy corridor where there is neither solvency nor bankruptcy; where the enmeshing of the taxpayer proceeds so slowly that he does not realize it; where the approaching woes of the creditor are hidden from him by operations of apparent safety; and where the capital is slowly whittled away by the pretense that the money will return from the labors of a certain posterity. This is heaven for the politician who now can be all things to all men: a creditor with creditors, a debtor with debtors, frugal with the taxpayer, and a source of profit for middlemen.

But the day will finally arrive with public debt where the politician must leave this pleasant pasture and decide where he will stand in an emergency. Because sooner or later all public debt will appear abruptly in the form of taxes, or will be repudiated. It may take years to reach this alternative, depending on many factors that cannot be foreseen. But, the alternative is inevitable.

When our government borrows against the future, it is gambling that there will be uninterrupted growth in the wealth that will make repayment possible. But in our times debt with 8% compound interest, as noted, this is totally illusory.

Beyond that, if we can judge from history no country can enjoy an unbroken march of progress in production. It is not in the cards. Nothing is more certain than the advance from adversity to prosperity or, like now, the decline from prosperity to adversity.

The character of human beings strengthens in periods of hard times and struggle, and declines under the security of prosperity as we have seen in America, especially since 1980. So, it can be said with absolute assurance that any contracts made by governments, and especially those made in respect to money, which go far into the future for their performance will never be performed according to the spirit in which they were made. Either conditions will have changes so much that a later generation regards a repudiation as common sense, or economic affairs make repayment impossible. Public debt regards only its own emergencies; it ignores the fact that every generation will have crises of its own—just like America has now.

The quantity of borrowing upon public credit generally coincides with the quantity of private borrowing. When individuals are squandering, governments are lavish, as we can see in America from our recent past. So, when debtors are in distress, indebted governments will share that distress. Every relief given to an individual then will equally disburden the state. Party lines also disappear at this time and everyone is either a creditor or a debtor.

The politician is the poor man's friend. If contracts were made, they are now regarded as scraps of paper. There is talk about human rights; the insolence of property, hungry children, unfair distribution of wealth; and the need for something new. It all aims for one thing: to spoil the debtor. Politicians have at long last come into their own. Public debt which they have grown and potted and repotted has at last flowered into…a crisis. That we all know now. But will political promises stem social turmoil?

Final note: Historically, the collapse of a monarchy due to state bankruptcy resulted many times in a parliamentary government. But the collapse of a democracy from the same cause leads often to dictatorship. And he who aspires to power in times of stress can take no straighter course toward his own design than to convince the distressed public debtors that he will cancel or alleviate debts, by any method he can contrive.

THE MUDDY POOL OF CREDIT

The average man stares helplessly at the pool of credit in which he is swimming. This pool is opaque because of the stirrings of economists and by those whose profits depend on the clouding of fundamentals.

The fundamentals governing the use of debt are simple. When a person borrows money or goods, he is entering into a contract; in the contract the promisor has curtailed his freedom of action; credit and debt are the same things under two different names; that the distress of an unfortunate debtor is of no real importance to the state; that the state puts paramount importance that contracts should be performed; and, that if wealth is mortgaged faster than it is being produced, like it has been in America for a very long time, then there must be a repudiation of contracts with a deflation of debt.

This should be plain. But now introduce the idea that when you take on debt, you are adding to the community's wealth, and you have created a picture to which a million optimists will flock, but out of which most of them will tumble, disillusioned, seedy or sullen.

There are grave dangers of continuously mortgaging expected wealth. Why don't people understand that: 1) if future production is late, the creditor will fly for security of his money, 2) if expected production fails, both lender and borrower lose, and 3) if a mountain of such contracts is pledged against what proves to be a fictitious hill of wealth, wholesale panic and depression will be the inevitable results.

So, we muddy the waters, and call debt credit. And we should speak of public credit for what it is: spending power the government has, and that it has nothing to do with taxation. Beyond that, call common stocks securities, and think of bonds as commitments. If this is done, this will create a vast complexity in the mind of the average man concerning the simple fact of borrowing, then he will come to regard himself as rich exactly to the extent that he can go into debt. Make the bud thick. But we must complain of the inevitable compensation: that both debtor and creditor will fall headlong into the same gutter.

To think that our present extraordinary public debts can be extinguished by government economy would be to imagine incomes tremendously increased, but not prices; where we all spent more, but thrift was larger; where machinery multiplied, but unemployment did not happen; above all imagine that the exchange between labor for labor was perfect. If you can imagine all of this, then imagine Paradise because that is where you would be.

Looking now at the turbulent, frustrated angry, and demoralized America, and where the only certainty we have left to us seems to be the assurance that whatever is about to happen next will prove to be unpleasant. For in the declines of economies, there is no one cause. But the natural repercussion of debt at every level upon our national character and attitudes, upon our morals and our laws, as well as upon the true economic welfare of men could possibly be the one event that pitilessly surrounds us and destroys us?

THE THREAT OF DEBT REPUDIATION

As the American economy continues to contract, the problem of servicing public debt will grow because there will be less income taxes and higher debts to fund public relief.

Then we face a historic dilemma: How will the federal government manage the problem without repudiation? Can they alter repayment terms of the outstanding debt such as transforming a 90-Day Treasury Bill into a 30-year repayment and avoid default for awhile?

Any signal that the government was trying to alter the terms of paying back its debt would cause foreign debt holders to swiftly sell their debt en masse—worsening the problem.

What if federal debt repudiation cannot be avoided? Then large debt owners, banks, corporations, and wealthy individuals would be wiped out, but also there would be no funds for Social Security and the many other sources of government payments. And so on.

The consequences of repudiation would create social unrest, turmoil with money, chaos. The threat of this future event is discussed in the next chapter.

Is there some other easy solution? Some way we can mollify the public and owners of debt? Probably not. We cannot reinvent the money wheel.

WHY DID PUBLIC DEBT EXPLODE?

In America—and in the world—public debt levels have exploded. Why should this happen after many, many years of budgets that were fairly closely in balance? However measured, debt grew, and the share of debt in the gross national product grew rapidly.

With Great Depression I far behind us by the late 1980s, memories of frugality, thrift, and saving likewise disappeared at all levels in American society. As a nation the stigma of debt vaporized. We were encouraged to "buy now and pay later." Living on the cuff became the "American Way." So, it was only natural that policymakers borrowed and borrowed and consistently ignored debts (at compound rates of interest) because, heretofore in America, the country had always been creditworthy and it was easy to borrow. And besides, debts in the past had a way of becoming irrelevant. Or so the economic experts thought. A whole school of economists emerged who theorized that debts were virtuous, that we owed the debts to ourselves and so we were simply transferring resources from one hand to another. Most of the economists making these flawed visions were themselves mathematicians by training. It is positively amazing that they, of all people, should have also ignored the extraordinary and terrible consequence of compound interest on the growing debt burdens. But they did, and here we are.

The role of government in society grew like topsy. Conventional wisdom stated the government should intervene, without end, to create jobs, spend for defense, go into space, and manage the distribution of income through various tax law changes and manipulations.

The intervention by the government was feverishly pushed outward. This phenomena was predicted many years ago by Oswald Spengler in the *Decline of the West,* and Arnold Toynbee in the *Study of History.* All through human history, governments have a built-in desire to expand their own power, roles, functions—governmental bureaucracy always takes on a life of its own and is ever present in governments of all sorts. But there was another reason for this expansion:

The consuming masses came to believe that they were entitled to various forms of cheap or free health care, transport, and other public services. But there was a disparity between the private cost of using these services and the social cost of providing them. This disparity brought enormous and growing burdens on the federal budget. Those who had the most to gain from the services—like the older population who collected Social Security benefits—were also large and politically powerful groups, and those who opposed them were small. Politicians, knowing where votes come from, courted the most voters and favored their benefits. So if the growing cost of providing these services had been covered by ordinary revenue, it would have meant a process of redistributing income in favor of lower-income users and, therefore, not incurring federal deficits.

While the voters approved higher spending, they would not support paying for it with higher taxes. As this process continued, the gap between government spending and income grew and this process accelerated federal deficit growth.

All through economic history, the reality behind continued deficit financing has been ignored. It has always been true, for example, that deficits are not to be assumed for investments that would be unproductive. After all, the main theory of going into debt is to assume that it will produce wealth which will repay the debt and allow society to grow. This is alas true for governments and true for the public as well.

However, this historic principle was evilly abandoned in favor of deficit financing which focused the public's attention on the goal of full employment, regardless of the cost, and expanding welfare programs with the very same flawed thinking processes. So, large and growing federal deficits paved the way to achieve these goals, and the devil was left to take the hindmost.

Beyond that, one of the old economic theories stated prominently was that governmental deficits in depressed times were justified in order to provide work and make-work, thus turning the economy around by creating demand. Lord Keynes was one of many economists to propose this. But a new dimension in our general outlook altered all of that: as a nation we began to take deficits for granted since we forgot that debts must be repaid. Most of the public was busy living beyond their own means by also borrowing for everything they wanted, so they ignored their government that was also borrowing heavily. We all thought something miraculous would happen and that debts would go away. But few realized that the double-double-process of compound interest would not allow this to happen. As the European Banker Rothschild is supposed to have said, "Compound interest is the 8th Wonder of the World." And it is. Ignorance of this power will prove fatal for America.

There were other factors, of course, that contributed to public debts exploding. The oil price rise in the 1970s caused real incomes to fall and the capital of various energy-intensive industries to become obsolete almost overnight. Many governments expected quick recovery which did not meet this challenge, but instead chose to borrow their way through the crisis rather than pursue the painful adjustment process. This was easy because the oil price rise created huge pools of savings in the OPEC countries that were seeking investments. So, the higher spending needs of governments were met by higher foreign borrowings (like the Latin nations did).

These borrowed funds created an enormous—global—pool of credit-dollars and their spending, in turn, raised the general prices creating an inflation that was sharp, but short-lived. As it waned, the decline in prices was slow. But the slowdown was not perceived to be "the end of inflation." Rather, as late as 1989, most Americans were still "fighting inflation." Prices rose without end for a different reason: the borrowing process created debts on which interest was paid. At a level of $12 trillion in domestic debt in America and at an interest rate of 10 percent, the interest costs alone were $1.2 trillion a year. Since interest is a cost of doing business, the higher costs were buried in prices and passed through to everyone throughout the system, thus causing prices to ratchet up year after year, creating an "inflationary illusion." But it was truly based on paying interest costs. The only way prices could fall was to have debts go into liquidation. When the interest costs disappear, the prices for the things we all buy and use finally fall, as they are now.

There were other by-products of the financial inflation. It caused a temporary reduction in real rate of interest (that is the true cost of interest after inflation is deducted) and this briefly reduced the ratio of public debt to national income. So, governments then thought they could borrow without future "pain."

What few understood was that it was the increased rate-of-change in inflation, rather than the inflation itself, that caused this fall in the real interest rate. Individuals began to adjust to inflation by avoiding financial assets with long maturities and fixed rates, or by buying assets indexed to price rises. Then the real rate of interest started to rise again. By the late 1970s, it was rising rapidly. The lesson unlearned that is the public will always, given time, adjust to inflationary policies.

It was during the 1960s, before the inflation, when America had significant real growth and when social programs were put in place. It was believed, of course that high growth rates would continue without end and this would generate the resources to finance the higher public spendings. But in the decade of the 1970s, growth slowed down sharply and the so-called "entitlements," created in the 1960s, took a larger proportion of the larger resources. So, as ordinary revenues fell, the increases in spending could only be financed by more borrowing. It was impossible to get off the public debt treadmill. And so they grew rising from 28 percent of GNP in 1972, to 35 percent in 1983, to 38 percent in 1989.

DEFICITS AND GROWING DEBTS

While all of this was going on, policymakers and the public were focusing on current federal deficits instead of the vast accumulation of liabilities by the Federal Government. Deficits were thought to be "temporary" and would affect us one year, but not the next. The cumulative effect of an endless chain of federal deficits was ignored by policymakers in Washington—they kept on borrowing. It is true that a deficit may make one year better, but it will be harmful next year if it leads, which it did, to a cumulative increase in total public debt (which it also did).

But deficit spending is thought of only as a short-term event. The growing total debt load was ignored. The exponential growth of interest was also ignored. When Ronald Reagan became President in 1980, the interest on federal debts was $69 billion a year. When he left office in 1988, it was $169 billion a year. The uncontrolled growth in the exponential function is ignored, but note the impact in this chart. Anything that grows as this double-double rate will finally destroy itself. That is why interest compounding is a financial nuclear bomb, and why it will bring ruin to all of us in America.

Figure 31: Federal interest payments, in billions of US dollars, as conservatively calculated by the US authorities and presented in January 1984.
Source: Congressional Budget Office

Cyclical deficits—those that grow in recessions and went into surplus in recoveries—were totally ignored. They were irrelevant. Meantime, policymakers thought of a budget being only in equilibrium when full employment was achieved and, since this could not happen, debts grew and grew.

When the rate of economic growth in America was high (as it was in the 1960s and after the end of World War II), and the level of the deficit was still small, then the share of public debt to GNP might not rise, even fall. The comparison between debt and GNP is made because, in theory, debts are paid out of the GNP. Gross National Product is the wealth produced by America. If not enough wealth is produced, debts cannot be paid. By 1990, GNP was about $4 trillion and debts were then over $12 trillion, so there were not enough resources left in America to pay back the debts, as anyone could see now. This vast discrepancy was ignored by the public.

NATIONAL BANKRUPTCY LOOMS

The consequences of this cumulative growth of federal debt levels with their accompanying compound interest loads will undermine our society, as I detail in a later chapter. We will face national bankruptcy. We simply cannot repay the debts we have incurred. Why not just write them off as unpaid? That would be the end of credit and prevent its further use, in addition to destroying the owners of the debt paper. The historic solution to debts is that they are always paid: either they are paid or they are defaulted, and this idea goes back to Biblical times.

DEBT GROWTH SPEEDS UP

The combination of our huge and rapidly growing public debt, coupled with high real rates of interest, made interest payments the fastest growing component of public spending. In the United States, interest payments as a percent of GNP rose from 1.5 percent in 1972 to 3.6 percent in 1986. Of course the growth of interest swells the public debt and makes it larger in the future. Public debts and deficits feed on themselves through the interest component of government spending. As the relative size of the debt increases, interest expenditure also grows. And, to make things worse, that growth can be accelerated, as it has been, by a rise in real interest rates or by a reduction in the rate of growth of the economy.

ECONOMIC GROWTH

We measure our national economic growth by measuring the growth rates of the Growth National Product. In the 1960s, GNP growth averaged 3.9 percent; in the 1970s, 2.8 percent; and from 1980 to 1986 the rate fell to 2.0 percent. So, in sum, the economy has been slowing down significantly since 1960, but public debts have soared, rising from $290 billion in 1960 to $2.5 trillion in 1986, almost ten times.[15]

Debt as percentage of GNP: In 1980 the federal debt was $930 billion, about 35 percent of the GNP. By 1983 it had surged to $1.4 trillion, or 43 percent of GNP. By the end of 1989 it was over $2.5 trillion, 55 percent of GNP.

So we have a deadly cycle of more debt, more interest, and less income to repay what is owed. This is a dangerous set of affairs and frightening for all Americans since it portends upheaval of the ongoing economic system.

WHAT ARE THE RESULTS OF TOO MUCH DEBT?

The financial effects are: 1) As the quantity of bonds to be sold increases, their price must fall, thus raising the market rates of interest. 2) The interest component of public spending rises and, consequently, increases future deficits themselves. 3) Because of 1 and 2, the effect on investment and consumption themselves changes the future consumption patterns of the economy and its future performance—investing more for consumption purposes than production purposes, for example. 4) These vast sums alter the exchange rate values and, in turn, trade flows and capital movements. 5) And the most dangerous effect: the *growing risk that things may go wrong.* And they surely are now as we all can see around us.

The risk increases when the total borrowing needs by the government become too large a share of total financial transactions, and this alters the psychology on Wall Street and in the global financial markets where the debts must find funds to support them. This enhances the harsh reality that some event can change good times to bad times in the minds of traders, causing them to dump securities in a panic.

GROWTH OF DOMESTIC DEBTS

Since American domestic federal debts have grown as a share of GNP, as shown above, it is inevitable that some private borrowing must be reduced unless foreign debts can be expanded. But, it was the foreigners willing to buy U.S. government debts that made the growth continue up until now and allowed private U.S. borrowing to continue as well as domestic consumption.

But the danger of that is that America has lost control of its financial destiny. Like any other debtor, we were forced to pay homage to our creditors, lest they lower the boom and withdraw their financial support, then sell their holdings, and destroy our financial markets in that process.

Bad as that possibility is, it would be worse: a growing fear of national lack of "creditworthiness"—*the fear that there would be no way the government could pay back its own debts.*

Accumulated public debt may induce psychological reactions that can make affairs even worse, if those who hold the debt think the government will attempt to change the ground rules one way or another. Any untoward action by authorities would provoke owners of debt to dump them and precipitate a colossal crisis. So, we face a total and complete Catch 22.

It may be too late for policymakers to reduce other spendings or increase taxes. The spending cuts would run into huge public opposition, and, if taxes were raised, the private sector would then have less funds to repay their own private pyramids of debts, causing another crisis, much larger....

IGNORING THE PAST

It is perfectly natural for policymakers to continue to live the American Dream that "things will always get better," that economic growth can be reignited, and so on. But this has not been happening now for almost twenty years. The basic and fundamental cycle changed, but public thinking did not. Why?

Fernand Braudel wrote:[16]

"Do we have the rare and unenviable privilege of seeing with our own eyes the century begin its downturn? If so, the short-term policies admirably directed towards immediate ends, advocated by our political leaders and economic experts, may turn out to be powerless to cure a sickness of which our children's children will be very lucky to see the end."

He continued,

"The present crisis which refuses to grow away is more sinister, as if it cannot manage to show its true face, or find a label or a model which would explain it and reassure us. It is not so much a hurricane as a flood, with the water rising slowly but alarmingly, under a sky obstinately grew and waterlogged. All the foundations of economic life and all the lessons of experience past and present seem to be now challenged."

CHAPTER NINE

REFERENCES

1. Aaron & Bendiner, *The Strenuous Decade* (Doubleday, N.Y.C., 1970), p. 74.

2. Mayer, Martin, *Wall Street Journal,* April 24, 1989, p. 37.

3. Hahn, L. Albert, *Economics of Illusion* (Squire Publishing, N.Y.C., 1949).

4. *Wall Street Journal,* April 29, 1989, p.2.

5. Brinton, Christopher, Wolf, *A History of Civilization,* Volume I, II (Prentice Hall, Englewood Cliffs, NJ, 1976).

6. Brinton, Christopher, Wolf, *A History of Civilization,* Volume I, II (Prentice Hall, Englewood Cliffs, NJ, 1976).

7. *World Link Magazine*, September-October, 1989, p. 11.

8. *Barron's,* September 11, 1989.

9. *Global Finance Magazine,* March 1990.

10. Groceclose, Elgin, *Money and Man* (University of Oklahoma Press, Norman, OK, 1934).

11. Hyman, Sidney, *Marriner S. Eccles* (Stanford University Graduate School Business, Stanford, CA, 1976).

12. *Economic Report of the President, 1988,* Tables B-1, B-68.

13. American Educational League, pamphlet, April 1990, Buena Park, CA.

14. *Economic Report of the President, 1987.*

15. *Economic Report of the President, 1987.*

16. Fernand Braudle, *Perspective of the World* (Harper and Row, New York, NY, 1984).

CHAPTER TEN

IS THE INTEREST PAYMENT SYSTEM FAIR?

Something must be inherently wrong with our economic system if, in its operation, it continually throws the public from good times to bad times such as we are witness to now. This swing has been a trait of capitalism since its beginning—from the beginning of it good times have been followed by hard times and no solution has ever arisen to this problem. We make the same mistakes over and over again. Therefore, there must be something built-in to the system that whips the system around. There must be something that causes these endless crises.

Capitalism is an economic system based on what is called "free enterprise" and with the adoption of the idea of private property provides rewards for economic risk and performance as well as individual responsibility for losses and damages. The notion of free enterprise, private property, performance and economic responsibility constitute the overwhelming advantages of a free economy. It is rightly true that because of these fundamental principles that western industrial economies have proven themselves to be so highly productive and efficient over the long-term.

Regarding economic performance and holding people responsible for what they do is not only sound economics, it is also ethically fair and just. Without this only the lazy would be privileged, and the rest of us would have to pay for the mistakes and leisure of those who would be living at our expense. So far as principles are concerned, capitalism does, indeed, outperform other forms of economic systems economically as well as with regard to the ethical standards of fairness and justice.

Despite these virtues, capitalism has some fatal flaws: in the long run it generates chronic unemployment. It cannot establish a satisfying welfare structure for the distribution of wealth among the members of the economic community. In advanced capitalism such as the present time, the arena of money and finance is far more powerful—and dangerous—that of real economic production, exchange and consumption. This vast expansion of debt, which is modern money, works and grows like a plague on the system since it cannot continue without precipitating panics and crashes. We have had an array of them since 1800 to give us proof of this fatal weakness. Capitalism is condemned to the economic disparities of continuing crises and disequilibrium.

Though capitalism promises free enterprise and private property and rewarding economic performance and, therefore, fairness, efficiency and justice, in the real world capitalism has not, over the years, been able to deliver these expectations to the general public. It fosters and tolerates, instead, large degrees of homelessness, crime and sheer poverty and leaves minorities to root through its ashes.

Is it safe, then, to assume that there is some hidden defect in the capitalistic system which curbs its output, and obstructs its economic process despite the system's seeming sound foundation?

Because of a hidden defect which has a powerful counter-productive force on total economic output, this fatal flaw is incompatible with capitalism's own fundamental principle of efficiency. So, it seems, it might be possible to eliminate the hidden defect of capitalism without harming its sound principles, thereby increasing its performance with regard to efficiency, welfare and fairness.

RETURNS ON YOUR MONEY

An integral part of capitalism is that it allows for income which does not come from risk, but from the simple, passive ownership of capital alone. And this specific income from capital grows at an accelerated rate because of compound interest or other kinds of re-invested returns. But over time in our society we have learned to perceive this to be our reward for our past work, and giving us a return on our savings for our retirement income. This is a major reason that we all favor the payment of interest since we think of it as "natural." We worked and saved so the financial system is obligated to take care of us with a return on our savings. This is believed by the public to be the way the system is supposed to work. Money interest and other capital revenues are part of our economic second nature and belief systems. The returns from interest are taken as legitimate beyond any doubt. So, it is unthinkable to question whether this revenue and interest is right for the economic performance of our entire economic—capitalistic—system. We all participate in this system, and we like it. And we do not want to think of, or question, changing these historic arrangements. Anything else is too foreign to our conscious and subconscious belief systems.

The stream of income which comes to you as an owner of capital comes from other members of the system. A young businessman, for example, who starts a business using borrowed money has to share his profit with the lender of the money even if the lender does not share the effort nor the risk. This, we think, is perfectly all right—the way capitalism should and must work.

So, it is designed into the positive interest reward system that there should be some kind of a negative reward for the businessman who does not abstain from business but who instead gets involved in economic risk and performance. And these negative rewards—paying interest—are transferred from the owners of capital who do not engage in the business but, by abstaining from their own activities, release their funds to be used by others, whether through the banking system or as individual lenders. They release funds they do not need right now, but these funds that are greatly needed by others.

Obviously, then, returns on money actually flow from someone who patently has substantial need of capital now to someone else who obviously has plenty of excess money at his disposal. Thus, interest transfers money from where it is used will be huge, to lenders where its use is always so low that the funds are excess to their owners, at least for a period of time. "Finance capital" is constantly and automatically being transferred from a place where its use is large to a place where its use is dispensable by its owners.

Naturally, borrowing money for producing something—starting a business—directs funds to where they are needed. In sum: money is lent where it is not needed to where it is needed, so the process is good. But the stream of interest represents a countertransfer of capital in the opposite direction. That is, from a level of high use (the new business venture) to a level of low use (the lender). So, this tendency throws a shadow on the ability of this type of economic system to be the best type of economic system. We think it is, but is it?

A return on idle capital (your funds) seems to be perfectly all right to the limited and select few who have accumulated these resources. But to the businessman that needs to borrow funds, this system is only second best. It also is second best for the majority of Americans who are striving to have the best, the very best, economic system for themselves.

It is not just theory, but a reality that money and commodities should have equal use to everyone. Instead, the way it is now it creates a counterstream of return on capital from high users to low levels of use. Since debt-money is used by so many different individuals in our vast economic system, with billions of transactions taking place each day, it is difficult to compare the use of money in each different individual case.

RETURN ON IDLE CAPITAL

The return on idle capital is, of course, perfectly all right and proper to the present owners of capital. After all, they truly believe, that is the proper way for capitalism to work. But for the nation as a whole, it is second best since our national goal should be national financial health. We should aim for equal opportunity of all our commodities and money instead of having a design which increases the disparities by using a counterstream of returns on capital from high to low levels of use.

There is no doubt that the use of any good is high for a person or a business if he is ready to pay a high price for holding it, that is if he is willing to burden himself with the financial burden in order to get the money he wants and needs. There is no doubt that the marginal use of a good to an individual is relatively small if he only prefers the use of the goods to holding other goods. That is, if he would not hold it if it burdened him with a real lack of use. So, exchanging money or commodities from people who are ready to pay a price for holding them to others who would not pay for them at all means transferring to the latter from a level of high use and need to a level of low use and need.

But an optimum system should equalize the cost and benefits of its commodities and its money. This means that in each case the real efforts and costs on the one hand the the real use and earnings on the other hand should balance each other. However, in our capitalistic society neither holds true. If you apply the readiness to accept the real cost to get the use of a good as the measure, neither do commodities and money tend to render equal use to individuals, nor do costs and benefits at the margin of capital tend to compensate each other.

HABITS OF THOUGHT

We believe in three capitalistic dogmas:
1) The productivity religion: we think that the efficiency or

technological productivity of physical plants and equipment (which we call capital) as such justifies a rate of return to capital above zero instead of a declining one.

2) The time-preference dogma: we believe that a preference for present over-deferred consumption justifies a money-rate of interest above zero. In other words, if you want a new car now and cannot pay cash for it, then it is all right to buy it and pay interest on the loan, a rate above zero, a rate in the late 1980s of 12 or 14%. This is perceived to be all right and ethical.

3) The return-to-property idea: we think it is all right and proper for the returns on capital not to flow back to the producer, the active user, but to the idle owner of capital.

The notion of an "idle owner" is not a radical idea. In an advertisement in the *Wall Street Journal,* November 15, 1989, Kemper Money Market Fund wrote, "How Old Money Gets That Way: The idle rich may be idle, but don't assume their money is. If you could look behind the scenes, you'd see that Old Money, the kind that's passed on from generation to generation, is usually in the hands of expert money managers. That's why the rich can be idle and still be rich."

There is a long-lived delusion in capitalism known as "pennies from heaven"—the widely held dream of getting something for nothing. It is true that the magic of debt-money and its self-multiplication make this possible for a very limited few—the rich.

Lord Keynes questioned Idea Number One above when he wrote, "It is much preferable to speak of capital as having a yield over the course of its life in excess of its original cost, than as being productive."

Why are the returns of productive capital expected to flow back to the owner according to the return-to-property dogma? Wouldn't it be better to reward the producer who takes the risk and is the creator? Would it not be better to pay higher prices directly to the skilled producers instead of rewarding the idle owner of capital?

Regarding the time-preference: why do individuals have to pay interest at a common rate for present over deferred investment or consumption even when the present specific real goods demanded are already relatively plentiful?

In the real world the returns on capital (interest) transfers resources from those high on the income plateau to those low on the plateau. Therefore, it is safe to assume there will always be a shortage of capital unless the tide can be turned from the present permanent drain of capital from where it is really needed to where it is hardly needed at all.

The implication is now perfectly clear: increasing amounts of money are always in the hands of the "capitalist" and others always lack capital. There is a tendency to back the needs of the wrong people and these unusual streams of income automatically lead to inadequate demand. And demand from others is being choked off because of lack of money. The result is that in the real world our capitalistic system tends to produce goods and service for the well-to-do, and in the long run increasingly fails to serve the needs of the less well-to-do members of the society: a surplus of expensive hotels and office buildings and palatial homes was a widespread phenomena on the American landscape in the late 1980s was proof.

Every financial asset owned by a creditor yields him positive returns, and this is equal to the negative return of the debtor with his negative financial asset, and this automatically increases disparities in wealth in all societies where the role of interest is large.

So, in the real world, capitalism is counterproductive in that it produces this habitual disparity of income between those who control self-growing capital and those stricken by a form of self-growing poverty. This poverty contrasts bewilderingly to the performance of the rest of the capitalistic economic system.

It is simple to prove that capitalism as it exists:

1) Widens the gap between the rich and the poor.
2) Misallocates credit so those that lack it pay more and

more interest.

3) Creates unbalanced flows of credit dollars.

An old economic observation was one by economist A.C. Pigou, who wrote many years ago, "The distribution of income in all societies in all ages remains the same within a narrow range." In other words, there have always been the rich and the poor, but the large role of interest absolutely prevents any balanced distribution of income. Any attempts to close the gap in income distribution with federal or private insurance plans, other income transfer systems, etc., are doomed to failure because of the toll interest takes off the top.

Why is it that the American masses seem to like the income disparity? The central reason, it seems to me, is that every person in America believes that the society provides a genuine chance for everyone to become rich—rags to riches is an old American theme and dream. So, if there is some financial suffering on the road to this goal, then it is accepted as being the price we must pay. If the goal is never achieved, people blame themselves as underachievers and do not blame the skewed economic system.

UNEMPLOYMENT MUST BE ENDEMIC

In an economic system where there is an ongoing transfer of financial resources from where they are really needed to where they are dispensable, there will always, because of this spread in cash flows and income, be needs that will remain unfinanced because of the system induced shortage of credit dollars. But one things is certain: the funds needed by those in need will not be delivered unless interest is paid. And the mere payment of interest worsens the misallocation. A Catch 22 has been created.

The result of this shortage of money to meet consumption needs, as well as money for production translates, very naturally, into rising unemployment—those who want to work and produce and invest cannot afford to do any of these functions because the credit dollars they need are too expensive for them to use.

IS DEBT MONEY EVIL?

Money enters into every economic activity. And this necessity is endangered because it can generate more money merely by owning capital. And the income it generates creates still more misallocations, further unbalancing the whole economic system.

If you want to buy anything, you must have the money first. You do not participate in the economy if you have no money. So, it is true: money buys goods and goods buy money, but goods do not buy goods.

Most often in America, most people do not have money at their disposal unless they first borrow it. If they borrow it, then they must pay interest, so they start out unfavorably. Not only that, they must pay interest during the entire period they have the loan.

SHOULD SAVINGS BE REWARDED?

The rate of interest cannot be a return to savings as such because if a man hoards cash, he earns no interest. The definition of the rate of interest is that it is a reward for parting with some of your "liquidity" for a certain period of time. Interest is the premium you get on current cash over deferred cash, so it measures all of our preferences for holding cash now or getting cash through future delivery.

So, interest is really not a positive reward; that is, a premium paid for abstaining from consumption. Instead, negatively, it is a premium for being passive and a punishment for your economic activity if you have to borrow. Some may object that loan money is credited to a borrower, but the credit is the main property of money as a way of exacting interest from borrowers. And it is not the default risk, as is commonly believed, that is main property of money that creates interest because if there were no risk (which sometimes happens when loans are collateralized superbly), interest rates should fall to zero which they, of course, never do.

IS U.S.-STYLE CAPITALISM FOR EVERYONE?

In the wake of the upheaval in Eastern Europe and Russia, this question arose. In the *Los Angeles Times,* February 18, 1990, it said, "Whoever is right, fundamental American principles may deeply influence Eastern Europeans struggling to veer away from communism—whatever examples they choose to follow. That is because all leading industrial democracies adhere to such time-honored U.S. values as the belief in private property and the rule of law."

So, the delusion continues.

NOW: THE POWER OF COMPOUND INTEREST

In the heady days of the 1980s a noted mathematical stock trader, who made a personal fortune of over $100 million, explained his trading techniques as follows: "Suppose you were to trade for thirty-five years at twenty percent return. Your money will multiply by a factor of five hundred and ninety. At ten percent return, say, it will multiply only by a factor of twenty-eight. You will have twenty-one times as much money with only twice the growth rate. That's why one of the barons Rothschild call compound interest the eighth wonder of the world. It is quite amazing."[1]

And the same power of interest compounded works for the lender and against the borrower...and has from Biblical times.

IN THE REAL WORLD

Sir Josiah Stamp, former President of the Bank of England had this to say about the banking business, where many of the interest bearing loans originate, "The modern banking system manufactures money out of nothing. The process is perhaps the most astounding piece of sleight of hand that was ever invented. Banking was conceived in iniquity and born in sin. Bankers own the earth. Take it away for them, but leave them the power to create money, and, with a flick of a pen, they will create enough money to buy it back again. Take this great power away from them and all great fortunes like mine will disappear [he was said to be the second richest man in Great Britain at that time], and they ought to disappear, for then this would be a better and a happier world to live in. But, if you want to continue to be the slaves of bankers and pay the cost of your own slavery, then let bankers continue to create money and control credit."[2]

CHAPTER TEN

REFERENCES

1. *Omni.*

2. *Money Talk,* June 25, 1987.

CHAPTER ELEVEN

LONG AND FORGOTTEN PRACTICE OF USURY

Probably not one American in ten knows, or cares, what "usury" is. According to *Webster's Dictionary,* usury is "The act of lending money at a rate of interest which is excessive or unlawfully high." How high is high?

About 1,000 years ago, Sidney Homer wrote a book about interest rate history and concluded that the average rate of interest for all of that period was 3.5%. That, and it is no coincidence, was the average growth rate of production, or what an average man can produce over time. So, the growth of interest rates higher than that meant that the worker was being "used," since he could not produce enough to pay off the compounding interest growth.

But there is another more real definition of usury, any profit, however great or little, taken for the loan of money.

Back in history, a form of thrift which collected usurious rates of interest was not held in the high esteem that it is today. If the ancients had little knowledge of the dynamic power of debt in commerce, the cultivation of which has resulted in a state where production, in order to exist at all, must be the fruit, not the basis, of a mortgage. Just three centuries ago theologians were still thundering against interest-taking as being akin, in sinfulness, to robbery, murder and incest, and fully supported the claim of Aristotle that money is naturally sterile and not honestly entitled to an increase.

If Aristotle's concept is a fallacy, how did it remain unchallenged for so long? And how was it so vigorously supported for so long?

As to the moral question in the taking of interest, there appears to have been unanimity among philosophers and later among theologians. Back in the days of the Romans and Greeks, it was denounced but it went on. The money-lender for profit has always been despised—and tolerated.

Money, many believe, has no value except its usage, and being consumed in the usage, and being incapable of producing anything by itself, it is merely an inert thing borrowed for the purpose of commanding capital goods. This being achieved, it is enough for the borrower to return the exact equivalent of the sum lent. The lender now has exactly what he had before in terms of exchangeable wealth, undiminished in power, like a horse that was returned whose capacity for work is limited. To get more than this loaned sum, said St. Thomas Aquinas, would be to ask pay for something which did not exist, or for a service that had not been performed.

Still another question came up when the creditor could show that in collecting interest for the use of his money, he was not doing so with the intent to profit, but merely to reimburse himself for an actual sustained loss. Theologians thought about this and then admitted a modification of the rule could be made to cover this.

John Calvin was a stout defender of usury who said that Aristotle nurtured a fallacy since money does not produce money but that which can be purchased with money does produce after its own kind. So, the arguments pro and con, and interest went on over the centuries until Henry VIII permitted by law money-lending at interest. And the Catholic Church thereafter made peace with this new world.

Once the bars were down an eager group of new-thought

economists walked through. There was a lot in the ancient conception of wealth and production as well as of the social order that was sharply challenged as business grasped the reigns for which it longed so long. The chief ferocity was directed towards the teachings of usury. Since then modern economists have taken issue with Aristotle and said that money was not sterile in artifices, but that it was sterile by nature. He did not say that money could not beget money, he said that in justice it should not. "Money," he said, "was devised for the exchanges but usury multiplies it." And this is not contrary to nature.

Jereyh Betham, the English economist/philosopher, hated the idea of usury and said that it did not make sense because of an increase in calves bought with borrowed money was an example of the wonderful workings of interest, should have recalled that cattle were producing long before money was invented, usury or no usury.

Economists now believe theologians invented and distorted and garbled to prove their usury assertions. The same might be charged against the economists who feel impelled to support the taking of interest upon loans as a moral procedure.

Jesus did not say a word to condemn usury, but neither did he condone it. He merely knew that it existed. Dante in the *Inferno* wrote:

"On the other hand, it must be said that unless the words 'lend hoping for nothing in return' are to be interpreted as a pronouncement of Jesus against usury, there is no condemnation of interest-taking in the New Testament."

Regardless of what has gone before, usury remains accepted today, aside from any moral position. It is not only all right, but it is revered by everyone.

It is not possible any longer to imagine someone saving today and not looking for his rightful yield on his investment.

This view does not negate the profound damage done by the collection of interest. The growing interest payments have made the total due run into astronomical sums that now cannot be paid back. Did we let it get too high? It does not matter. Perhaps now in the tumultuous change we are undergoing, it is the time to rid our money system of interest bearing debt-money. This is covered in another chapter.

RECENT AMERICAN USURY HISTORY

In America, interest payments as a percentage of national income increased from one percent in 1950 to nine percent in 1989, which placed a heavy load on the American economic system and the public as well. Amazingly, the burden of interest is invisible, and it is never seen as the wrecking machine that it truly is since interest is the reward for having excess funds work for the owner.

During the Great Depression, interest charges consumed profits. In fact, in 1932 and 1933 profits were negative. Back in the last Depression, the percentage of national income that was paid in interest charges doubled between 1929 and 1933. This was due in part to the price deflation back then.

It is theorized by some that the fall in real wages in America since 1973 has been due, in large part, to the sharp rise in interest payments. This phenomena has also been largely ignored by economists.

The enormous world debt problems are a part of the usury problem. If you borrow and can create assets which are greater than the value of the debt, then the loan is beneficial. But if the money loan is siphoned off into non-productive ventures, into the pockets of the politicians abroad (as happened in the Third World), then the debt burden for the economy increases sharply. This invites bankruptcy by the borrower, which is what European Kings did frequently in the fifteenth and sixteenth centuries.

Bankruptcy is one of the great inventions of capitalism. It provides an orderly way of getting rid of something which should have been gotten rid of and which politicians can never achieve except by elections and sometimes by revolutions.

Why does the public ignore the toll paying interest of debt takes? For the most part, it is artfully hidden from them because it is most frequently buried in the price of the things they buy. For example, in America in 1989, there was $12 trillion of domestic debt. At a 10% interest cost, this would mean $1.2 trillion a year must be paid in interest alone. How was it paid? Since interest is a cost of doing business, it was passed on to the public in the form of price increases, all along the line from producer to consumers. The price rises on average amounted to about 4%, and this was perceived to be "inflation" but it was "debtflation"—prices rising due to interest costs. And the public blindly paid the price asked and did not realize that they were really also paying interest costs. And so the interest bills were paid unknowingly by everyone. This artful process gave the practice of usury the nine lives it has had from the beginning of economic time.

CHAPTER TWELVE

A NEW KIND OF MONEY: ONE THAT IS DEBT-FREE

THE HIDDEN FLAWS IN OUR ECONOMIC SYSTEM

Something must be inherently wrong with our economic system if, in its operation, it continually throws the society from good times and into bad times like the present time. But, this is the long history of capitalism—from the beginning, good times have been followed by hard times and no solution has ever arisen to this problem. We make the same mistakes over and over again. Therefore, there must be something built-in to the system that whips the system around—some one cause that creates these endless crises.

Capitalism, an economic system based on what is called "free enterprise" and private property also has rewards for economic risk and performance as well as individual responsibility for losses and damages. The notion of free enterprise, private property, performance and economic responsibility constitute the overwhelming advantages of a free economy. It is rightly true that because of these fundamental principles that Western industrial economies have proven themselves to be so highly productive and efficient.

Regarding economic performance and holding people responsible for what they do is not only sound economics, it is also ethically fair and just. Without this, only the lazy would be privileged, and the rest of us would have to pay for the mistakes and leisure of those who would be living at our expense. So far as principles are concerned, capitalism does, indeed, outperform other forms of economic systems economically as well as with regard to the ethical standards of fairness and justice.

Despite these virtues, *capitalism has some fatal flaws:* in the long run it generates chronic unemployment. It cannot establish a satisfying welfare structure for the distribution of wealth among the members of the economic community. Right now the arena of money and finance overshadows that of real economic production, exchange and consumption. This money weakness is a plague on the system since it does not progress without panics and crashes. Capitalism is thus condemned to the economic disparities of of continuing crises and disequilibrium.

Though capitalism promises free enterprise and private property and rewarding economic performance (and, therefore, fairness, efficiency and justice, in the real world), capitalism has not, over the years, been able to deliver these expectations to the general public.

It is safe, then, to assume that there is some hidden defect in the capitalistic system which curbs its output and obstructs its economic process despite the system's seeming sound foundation.

Because of its counterproductive effects on economic output, this defect is incompatible with capitalism's own fundamental principle of efficiency. So, it seems, it might be possible to eliminate the hidden defect of capitalism without harming its sound principles, thereby increasing its performance with regard to efficiency, welfare and fairness.

RETURNS ON MONEY

Capitalism allows for income which does *not* come from risk, but from simple, passive ownership of capital alone. And this specific income from capital grows at an accelerated rate, with compound interest or other kinds of re-invested returns. But, in our society we perceive this to be the reward for our past work, having funds for our retirements, for example—we worked and saved so the system should take care of us and our money. This is thought to be a natural and a commonplace event in our system. Money interest and other capital revenues are part of our economic second nature and belief systems. The returns from interest are taken as legitimate beyond any doubt. So, it is unthinkable to question whether this revenue and interest is right for the economic performance of our entire economic—capitalistic—system. We live in it. We enjoy it. And we do not want to think of changing these historic arrangements. Anything else is too foreign to our natural order. *But interest is also an economic wrecking machine.*

The stream of income which comes to you as an owner of capital comes from other members of the system. A young businessman, for example, who starts a business using borrowed money has to share his profit with the lender of the money even if the lender does not share the effort nor the risk. This, we think, is all right—the way capitalism should and must work.

So, it is designed into the system that there should be some kind of a negative reward for the businessman who does not abstain from business but who instead gets involved in economic risk and performance. and these negative rewards—paying interest—are transferred from the owners of capital who do not engage in the business but, by abstaining from their own activities, release their funds to be used by others, whether through the banking system or as individual lenders. They release funds they do not need right now, but funds that are greatly needed by others.

So returns on money actually flow from someone who obviously has substantial need of capital now to someone else who obviously has plenty of excess money at his disposal. Thus, interest transfers money from where its use is huge, to lenders where its use is so low that the funds are excess to their owners, at least for a period of time. "Finance capital" is constantly and automatically being transferred from a place where its use is large to a place where its use is dispensable by its owners.

Naturally, borrowing money for producing something—starting a business—directs funds to where they are needed. Money is lent where it is not needed to where it is needed, so the process is good. But the stream of interest represents a countertransfer of capital in the opposite direction—that is, from a level of high use (the new business venture) to a level of low use (the lender). So, this tendency throws a shadow on the ability of this type of economic system to be the best type of economic system. We think it is, but is it?

A return on idle capital (your funds) seems to be perfectly all right to those few who have accumulated these resources. But to the businessman that needs to borrow funds, this system is only second best. And it is also second best for the whole American public who are striving to have the best, the very best, economic system.

It is not just theory, but a reality that money and commodities should have equal use to everyone rather than creating a counterstream of return on capital from high users to low levels of use. For so many different individuals it is difficult to compare the use of money by each different individual.

RETURN ON IDLE CAPITAL

The return on idle capital is, of course, perfectly all right and proper to the present owners of capital. After all, they say, that is how capitalism works. But for the nation as a whole it is second best since our national goal should be national financial health. We should aim for equal opportunity of all our commodities and money instead of having a design which increases the disparities by using a counterstream of returns on capital from high to low levels of use.

There is no doubt that the use of any good is high for a person or a business if he is ready to pay a high price for holding it, that is if he is willing to burden himself with the financial load in order to get the money he wants and needs. There is no doubt that the marginal use of a good to an individual is relatively small if he only prefers the use of the good to hold other goods. that is, if he would not hold it if it burdened him with a real lack of use. So, exchanging money or commodities from people who are ready to pay a price for holding them to others who would not pay for them at all means transferring to the latter from a level of high use and need to a level of low use and need.

But an optimum system should equalize the cost and benefits of its commodities and its money. This means that in each case the real efforts and costs on the one hand and the real use and earnings on the other hand should balance each other. However, in our capitalistic society, neither holds true. If you apply the readiness to accept the real cost to get the use of a good as the measure, neither do commodities and money tend to render equal use to individuals, nor do costs and benefits at the margin of capital tend to compensate each other.

HABITS OF THOUGHT

We believe in three capitalistic dogmas:
1) The productivity religion: we think that the efficiency or technological productivity of physical plants and equipment (capital) as such justifies a rate of return to capital above zero instead of a declining rate.
2) The time-preference dogma: we believe that a preference for present over deferred consumption justifies a money-rate of interest above zero. In other words, if you want a new car now and cannot pay cash for it, then it is all right to buy it and pay interest on the loan, a rate above zero, a rate today of 12% or 14%. This is perceived to be all right and ethical.
3) The return-to-property idea: we think it is all right and

proper for the returns on capital not to flow back to the producer, the active user, but to the idle owner of capital.

The notion of an "idle owner" is not a radical idea. In an advertisement in the *Wall Street Journal*, November 15, 1989, Kemper Money Market Fund wrote, "How Old Money Gets that way: The idle rich may be idle, but don't assume their money is. If you could look behind the scenes, you'd see that Old Money, the kind that's passed from generation to generation, is usually in the hands of expert money managers. That's why the rich can be idle and still be rich."

These ideas conform to the capitalistic "pennies from heaven" dream of getting something for nothing. The magic of money and its self-multiplication make this possible.

Lord Keynes questioned Idea Number One saying, "It is much preferable to speak of capital as having a yield over the course of its life in excess of its original cost, than as being productive."

Why are the returns of productive capital expected to flow back to the owner according to the return-to-property dogma? *Wouldn't it be better to reward the producer who takes the risk and is the creator?* Would it not be better to pay higher prices directly to the skilled producers instead of rewarding the idle owner of capital?

And regarding time-preference: why do individuals have to pay interest at a common rate for present over deferred investment or consumption even when the present specific real goods demanded are already relatively plentiful?

In the real world the returns on capital (interest) transfers resources form those high on the income plateau to those low on the plateau, hence there will always be a shortage of capital unless the tide can be turned on the permanent drain of capital from where it is really needed to where it is hardly needed at all.

The implication is clear: increasing amounts of money are always in the hands of the "capitalist" and others always lack capital. There is a tendency to back the needs of the wrong people and these unusual streams of income automatically lead to inadequate demand. And demand from others is being choked off because of lack of money. The result is that in the real world our capitalistic system tends to produce goods for the well-to-do and in the long run increasingly fail to serve the needs of the less well-to-do members of the society: a surplus of expensive hotels and office buildings and palatial homes was a widespread phenomena on the American landscape in the late 1980s is proof of this event.

Every financial asset owned by a creditor yields him positive returns, and this is equal to the negative return of the debtor with his negative financial asset, and this automatically increases disparities in wealth.

So, in the real world, capitalism is counterproductive in that it produces this habitual disparity of income between those who control self-growing capital and those stricken by a form of self-growing poverty—this poverty contrasts bewilderingly to the performance of the rest of the capitalistic economic system.

It is simple to prove that capitalism as it exists:

1) Widens the gap between the rich and the poor.
2) Misallocates credit so those that lack it pay more and more interest.
3) Unbalanced flows of credit dollars result.

An old economic observation was that of A.C. Pigou who wrote many years ago, "The distribution of income in all societies in all ages remains the same within a narrow range." In other words, there have always been the rich and the poor, but the concept of interest absolutely prevents any balanced distribution of income. Any attempt to close the gap in income distribution with insurance, social policies, etc., is doomed to failure.

Why is it that the American public seems to like the income disparity? The central reason, it seems to me, is that every person in America believes that the society provides a genuine chance for everyone to become rich—rags to riches is an old American theme and dream. So, if there is some financial suffering on the road to this goal, then it is accepted. If the goal is never achieved, people blame themselves, not the system.

UNEMPLOYMENT MUST BE ENDEMIC

In an economic system where there is an ongoing transfer of financial resources from where they are really needed to where they are dispensable, there will always, because of this spread in cash flows and income, be needs that will remain unfinanced because of the shortage of credit dollars. But one thing is certain: the funds needed by those in need will not be delivered unless interest is paid. And the mere payment of interest worsens the misallocation. A Catch 22 has been created.

The result of this shortage of money to meet consumption needs as well as money for production translates, very naturally, into rising unemployment—those who want to work and produce and invest cannot afford to do any of these functions because the credit dollars they need are too expensive for them to use.

MONEY: IS IT THE ROOT OF ALL EVIL?

Money enters into every economic activity. And this necessity is imperiled because it can generate more money merely by owning capital. And the income it generates creates still more misallocations, further unbalancing the economic system.

If you want to buy anything, you must have money first. You do not participate in the economy if you have no money. So, it is true: money buys goods and goods buy money, but goods do not buy goods.

Most often in America most people do not have money at their disposal unless they first borrow it. If they borrow it, then they must pay interest, so they start out unfavorably. Not only that, they must pay interest during the entire period they have the loan.

SHOULD SAVINGS BE REWARDED?

The rate of interest cannot be a return to savings as such because if a man hoards cash, he earns no interest. The definition of the rate of interest is that it is the reward for parting with some of your "liquidity" for a certain period of time. Interest is the premium you get on current cash over deferred cash, so it measures all of our preferences for holding cash now or getting cash through future delivery.

So, interest is not a positive reward, that is, a premium paid for abstaining from consumption but, instead (negatively), a premium for being passive and as a punishment for economic activity. Some may object that loan money is credited to a borrower, but the credit is the main property of money as a way of exacting interest from borrowers. And it is not the default risk, as is commonly believed, that is the main property of money that causes interest, because if there were no risk, interest rates should fall to zero, which they, of course, do not.

ECONOMIC GROWTH AND INTEREST GROWTH

It is no exaggeration to observe that interest grows much faster than topsy, or anything else for that matter. Note this data:

U.S. GROWTH: GNP AND INCOME

1946-1986

Real Gross National Product Increased	+235%
Money Gross National Product Increased	+1,881%
Employees Pay Increased	+1,981%
Corporate Profits Increased	+1,642%
Net Interest Increased	+16,283%

Source: Statistical Abstract, 1987.

A NEW KIND OF MONEY, ONE THAT IS DEBT-FREE

In the last forty years or so, money has taken on a life of its own. It became a force, like gravity and nature, and it flowed where and when it wanted to flow.

We have all seen its chain reaction powers, and this time on a global scale. A sudden financial crisis saw major center banks lose deposits at the speed of light. In an attempt to survive, they dumped their assets, bonds, and stocks, sending their prices crashing down. And then they called on the Federal Reserve Bank for additional credits to survive. This was because the Federal Reserve system was supposed to be "the bank of last resort," but it was not because the Federal Government itself had gone too far in debt. Also, the Federal Reserve System itself never had the financial resources it needed.

There was only one asset that everyone sought in the panic, that was gold. Bread lines in Detroit, grass growing on a street called Rodeo Drive in Beverly Hills, all of this chaos and more, and men still clamored for gold, bidding it to sky-high prices.

AN IMPORTANT CRISIS

The crisis we are now in speeds change in a society like ours which has never been static. Crises always force the acceptance of new points of view and of reforms long needed. Our past financial system had too many inadequacies which our current collapse has made so evident. We will now attempt to reform these inadequacies. The belief that reform can seriously be accomplished will be what differentiates our travail from that of the last Great Depression. Back then all efforts were made for the federal government to intervene to keep industrial capitalism alive.

Unlike, then, our capitalistic economic system, this time it will be weakened beyond repair, and odds favor the disappearance of the market-price system which included in the past some competition and some monopoly. We are relearning that there is no stability in our economic lives, that the only certain factor is continual change.

The terrific havoc depressions bring has shown light on the weakness inherent in a system which uses debt money for exchange and survival.

It is of no use to look reforms in our system such as those the New Deal of Franklin Roosevelt accomplished. This is because now the economic system called "capitalism" which Roosevelt saved is itself terminal. A new system is in the making to replace it.

Therefore, since the underpinning of capitalism was debt-money, the time has come to change this debt money into debt-free money. By so doing we can eliminate a major and fundamental flaw that existed and dominated the past economic structure.

DEBT-FREE MONEY

The idea of having a money system that does not include interest for the use of money is not new in economic history, though it may seem new to us now.

However, all the time the last economic boom was moving along, a number of people were beginning to think about the evils inherent in an economic system that used debt money as its main currency. Their focus centered on the absurdity of having to pay interest. The public was all so caught up in simply paying interest that few realized the final consequences of this phenomena, and what a wrecking machine it turned into...until now.

PENNIES FROM HEAVEN

Everyone knows the good the money does...it makes the wheels turn, and it buys things we all want. We all always want more since money is a power.

Although money allows you to buy what you want, it also can keep you from having those same goods because built into money is the payment of interest. This invisible device upsets the distribution of money and income distribution, giving more to those who lend than it does to those who borrow.

Why don't we pay any attention to interest? Because most times it is invisible; that is, its interest compounds and, although it is being recorded by computers on your accounts, you do to notice it until a payment is made and you find that most of your payment has gone to make the interest payment and little to pay the principal.

Why is this? Because of the nature of compounding and because interest grows exponentially. The best way to understand this is to think of what is known as the "Rule of 72." This is a mathematical way of explaining interest growing exponentially: let's say you pay 9%, for example, on a loan. Divide that into 72. Since it goes 8 times, the money doubles in 8 years; 12% doubles in 6 years, etc., 3% interest doubles in 24 years.

PATTERNS OF GROWTH

One of our problems in understanding the growth of interest— exponential growth—is that we confuse that form of growth with natural growth. The difference is shown in this chart:

BASIC TYPES OF GROWTH PATTERNS

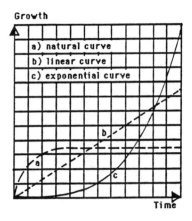

In no phase of normal development does exponential, undifferentiated growth take place.

However, exponential growth is something else. It is when, for example, things grow with a constant rate of compounding, like interest, or when a population grows when birth rate exceeds the death rate. Here the idea of "doubling time" is important. Again, at 7% annual growth rate, the doubling time is about 70 years.

So, to get a money system back on track, more in line with natural growth, there must be the creation of a new form of money: one that is debt-free, that carries no interest.

We have had the experience of undifferentiated growth and it resembles the growth of cancer. It is also similar to the type of world growth during the last generation. But making the transition is not a Doomsday Machine, but a dawn. A new beginning, not an end.

We had in our recent past crises in energy, food, materials, and money. The change to a debt-free form of money is a blessing in disguise. If we do not take this big step, then we will repeat our past financial mistakes. The recurring depressions are proof—twenty since 1800—that we must rid our system of its probable main cause: money that is interest bearing and not debt-free.

We have always paid interest in our society. This is because interest is a cost of borrowing money. In our society, everyone borrows, so when a business is granted a large loan at any rate of interest, the interest is a business cost and it is simply added back into the price of the good or service being produced. Thus, over time, a Coca Cola no longer costs 5 cents, but 50 cents. This cancer-like spread permeated our entire system. For example, in a gas or electric bill, the price of gas included the interest cost of the borrowed money that built the plant that brought the power, and so on. The payment of interest is truly cancer-like.

WHO PAYS INTEREST AND WHO COLLECTS IT?

Perhaps more than any one thing, the payment of interest and its collection is the main cause for the wide spread in the distribution of income in America. In studies of interest payments and the incomes from interest in equal sections of the U.S. population divided into ten groups, the first eight groups paid more interest than they received. The ninth group received a little more than it paid, and the tenth, or higher income group, received twice as much interest as it paid—getting the shares of the first eight. So the rich get richer and the poor, poorer.

So, the interest payment system operates as a hidden redistribution-of-income-device, taking money constantly from those who have less than they need and giving it to those who have more than they need. Over time, more and more money is concentrated in the hands of fewer people and corporations. This one single fact, more than any one thing, explains the long-term concentration and continual growth of "old money" fortunes in America, and why the early industrial-made fortunes are still with us and still growing. They will grow tomorrow unless the interest income system is changed.

But beyond that fact is the one that brought us Financial Doomsday. Government debts will sooner or later outgrow government income in every nation. Within the last few years in America, we were all witness to the rapidly and ever growing component of interest payments in the massive government debts.

The spread in incomes in America has been studied and restudied and tabulations of the richest men and women have always been with us. But it is interesting that with all of these mountains of studies of income distribution, the interest income of the rich and powerful was ignored.

But it goes deeper than that because a monetary system like that in America, which injects money into the economy in the form of debt-money, must collapse because the law of compound interest always causes debt and interest owed to accumulate faster than people can earn the income to pay it. A fatal flaw— and we have the current Depression to prove it.

REPLACING INTEREST PAYMENTS WITH A FEE

The idea of changing the monetary system and getting rid of interest was first described, to my knowledge, by Silvo Gesell in 1890. He proposed that money should be a government service subject to a use fee. Instead of paying interest to those who have more money than they need in order to bring money back into circulation, the public would pay a small fee if they kept money out of circulation.

Another common way of explaining this process is to compare money with a car on a train which carries freight. The railroad does not pay the user a premium to unload the train to bring the car back into circulation. Instead the user pays a small daily fee if he does not unload it. This is common practice in our society where we pay fees to others to "hold" something we want until we are able to pay for it.

We can do the same with money: when America issues "new" money in order that business activity can take place, it will, in the future, charge a small fee to the user who holds on to the new money longer than he needs for buying and selling purposes.

Interest now is a private gain. The new "fee" on the use of money would be a public gain. The fee would have to return into circulation in order to maintain the balance between the volume of new money issued and the volume of business activity. The fee would serve as income to the government and lower the taxes needed to carry out public works.

This idea was implemented in a small town in Austria in the 1930s. In Worgl, the residents agreed for the local authorities to issue 5000 "Free Schillings"—interest free Schillings—covered by the same amount of Austrian Schillings in the bank. They used the proceeds to build bridges, improve roads, etc., and paid salaries and those incomes everyone accepted in the community. The fee they devised on the use of the money was 1% per month, or 12% per year. This fee had to be paid by the person who had the banknote at the end of each month—being charged a "parking" fee—and the fee was shown by a stamp stuck to the note. If it did not have the stamp, the note was invalid. The public paid its taxes ahead of time to avoid paying the small fee. The economic effect: the 5000 Free Schillings circulated 463 times, thus creating goods and services worth 5,000 times 463, more than 2,300,000 Schillings. The ordinary Schilling by sharp contrast circulated only 213 times.[1]

During a period when most European countries were in hard times with high unemployment, this small town, Worgl, reduced its unemployment rate by 25% within one year. The fees collected by the town amounted to 12% of 5,000 Free Schillings—or 600 Schillings. This was then used for public purposes—no one individual gained from it, but rather the entire community.

This idea rapidly expanded to over 300 communities in Austria until the Austrian National Bank saw its money monopoly endangered. It intervened and prohibited the printing of private money.

Irving Fisher, the famed U.S. economist, tried to introduce Gesell's idea of cost bearing money into the U.S. in 1933. Back then 100 towns planned to issue stamp scrip. There was no objection from Washington authorities, but the project was finally turned down by a conservative economic advisor, Russel Sprague. When Roosevelt closed the banks on March 6, 1933, he ordered that no emergency currency could be issued. That ended the experiment.

BUT TODAY IT CAN BE DIFFERENT

Because 95% of our money today is on a computer, it would be very easy to put into effect a "use-fee." We would all have two accounts: one a checking account and one a savings account. The money in the checking account, which we are free to use at any time, would be treated like cash and would lose 1/2% per month, or 6% a year. So, anyone with more money in that account than they needed for current expenses would be tempted to transfer the excess to their savings account instead of paying the 6% annual fee.

For the savings balances, the banks (under Federal control) would be able to lend out these funds without interest to those who needed it, for a given time and, therefore, there would be no fee on the savings accounts.

Accordingly, the new money owner would not receive any interest on his/her savings account, but the new money would retain its value. It would not be lost to inflation. The person receiving the credit equally would not pay interest, but instead pay a risk premium and bank fees like those included today in all bank loans to cover operating costs, about 1.5%.

So there would not be much change from the present. One significant change would be the Federal operation of the banking system, removing it from private control through a nationalization process.

In the new Federal banking system, banks would operate as usual except that they would be more interested in making loans because they, too, would be penalized with the use fee if they did not.

So as to balance the amount of credits and savings available on a temporary basis, banks might have to pay or receive a small amount of interest, plus or minus 1%, depending on whether or not they had more new money in savings accounts than they needed or whether they had liquidity problems. Here the interest payment is distribution system as we had in the past.

After awhile the amount of money in circulation would meet the amount needed to conduct business. No more would then be created. Therefore, new money would follow the natural growth pattern of the human and not the exponential growth pattern of the past lenders and usurers.

The past interest bearing system (which has finally wrecked our economic system) was one where the lenders always loaned more since they collected the interest. They piled one debt on top of another…the mounting debt loads with compounding interest led to our colossal financial breakdown. Interest bearing money, as old as it is, has always been an evil instrument of torture for the consuming masses. Great for the lender and usurer, terrible for the borrower.

There could not be a better time to implement this new currency than now. It failed in the 1930s because the crisis was not deep enough. This crisis, one seemingly without end, will be so great and long lasting that a change of this sort should be most welcome by the public.

It is only one of many changes we are now living through, but it nonetheless is an important one for now and tomorrow.

CHAPTER TWELVE

REFERENCES

1. Kennedy/Dieter.

CHAPTER THIRTEEN

JUST MAYBE...THE END OF CAPITALISM AND THE INDUSTRIAL SOCIETY?

IS "CAPITALISM" ENDING?

Since the industrial society was born over 300 years ago, it has been believed up until now that the main goal of modern capitalism was the pursuit of profit, and that profits were made primarily in the industrial production of goods and the expansion of services. Hence the name to describe the system, "the industrial society."

This idea was so deeply entrenched that it was taught in economics courses in our universities and the role of producing goods for profit was placed on a pedestal. Vast data was accumulated to describe the health of our industrial society: Gross National Product, employment, sales of goods, and so on. It captured the public's attention because this production information was also the center point of business media information.

The main emphasis in the pursuit of profits has been shifted to financial-money-dealings and away from goods-money-dealings. Making goods had been the main source of American profits before 1900—an age also identified as by the era of the Robber Barons.

In other words, the industrial society had changed: the pursuit of profit was the driving force. It was soon learned by the profit-makers that there could be more profits made in making-money-activities, than in making-goods-activities. The society shifted to one that centered its attention on "juggling money," as noted earlier.

The emphasis on money "alone" is very old. It gave rise to the prominence of bankers, and the power of the usurer, the creditor far back in history. In 1989 in America, we had over $12 trillion in domestic debts to prove the overpowering influence of the financial men, the power of the creditors, the delusion of credit.

This emphasis on acquiring money transformed our society. Instead of stressing the family, religion, the work ethic, and other verities of the old industrial society, we all struck out for "more money"—the "deal." Like people in other nations before us and all through history, we believed that "more money" would promise a better life for all of us.

THE CREDIT DELUSION

In the long and involved history of political economy there is one word that stands out beyond all others as a triumph of imposture. That word is "credit." The perfect victory for this lying term in our economy has been reserved for the period from 1960 to 1990. The intent to delude the public by the use of the word goes back to the classical ages. Both the Greeks and the Romans were adept in the employment of euphemisms.

It is not possible to say at what time the word "credo" in Rome began to take on its present meaning, but two things are certain: the original meaning of the word referred to faith or trust that had nothing to do with the loan of capital, and also that there had been, since the earliest days, several words amply describing the loan of goods or money. But by the time of Cicero, it was either good taste or good business to place the cart in front of the horse; that is, to call a debt a credit, and to speak of "trusting" a many when "lending to him" was meant. There is no doubt in my mind that the fraudulent use of the word credit was perverted with the intent to delude—first by the lender of capital, then by the borrowers, and then by the entire economy.

And this perversion has succeeded. When we say we have "a line of credit" at the bank, we are proud. What if we said we "are in debt to the bank"? We speak of public credit and we instantly picture a vast amount of money in the public treasury. Say "public debt," which is the truth, and the taxpayer moans and groans. "Use your credit with us," the merchants cry out. They should say, "We will permit you to go in debt to us." Credit does not sound like something that must be paid. On the contrary, it has the ring of something that has been paid—a reward for integrity. Debt, on the other hand, is a mournful word, a gloomy word, a raven of foreboding. Debt is harsh. Credit sings like a nightingale. It is not odd that we speak of "enjoying" credit. But you have never heard of anyone "enjoying" debt—except the banker or insured creditor.

So, it has been easy to delude the public, as credit instruments have grown rapidly: credit cards (a sure-fire winner from the start), mortgage loans, car loan paper, lines of credit—and on and on. All bearing interest. The public became hostage to the creditor and, then, of course, emerged the debtor class—a nation hostage to the pursuit of money in order to pay debts was the final result. The public all the while thought their "credit" was okay. Now they are learning it has brought them ruin.

WHAT IS SO WRONG WITH THAT?

Perhaps the American public's greatest shortcoming was its inability to understand the exponential function designed into compound interest. Here's an example of the awesome power of exponential growth: if one penny had been invested at the birth of Jesus Christ at 4% interest, it would have bought by 1750 a ball of gold the weight of the earth. By 1990 it would buy 8,190 balls of gold. At 5% interest it would have bought one ball of gold already in 1403 and by 1990 it would buy 2200 billion balls of gold the weight of the earth. This example shows the difference 1% makes over a longer period of time. It also proves that the continual payment of interest and compound interest is arithmetically as well as practically impossible. This economic necessity, coupled with the mathematical impossibility, has created a contradiction whose thread runs all through history leading to wars, feuds, revolutions, and huge economic breakdowns.

The most insidious thing about exponential growth is that each doubling increases the number by as much as all its previous growth. By the time we realize that, the exponential growth of something has landed us in trouble and it may be too late to save ourselves from catastrophe.

It is easy to see why nothing real can grow, particularly at large percentages of itself for very long. It is why banks can't allow you to leave money with them for very long. Indeed it shows that the banking system repeatedly breaks down—because debts and interest on debts tend to increase faster than real or even money income can grow to repay them.

So, our banks have broken down and taken our funds with them, and we have been left rooting through the ashes as the era of credit money died in the flames of credit contraction and hard times.

THE END OF CAPITAL VALUES

The present value of an investment in a capitalistic society is calculated by discounting the future flow of income from it at the current interest rate. If that investment is projected to yield one dollar each year and the rate of interest is 10%, its present value will be the sum of a series beginning with 9/10 of $1 plus $1x(.90) plus $1x(.90) , and so on. High-school algebra will show that the sum of such a series is $10. Raise the interest rate to 20% and the value of the series will drop to $5.

In addition, the 20% interest rates, by depressing business activity, may reduce that one dollar of annual income and maybe even make it disappear. When the present value of an investment is less than the cost of the project, the investment no longer makes sense. If it has already been made, it will have only scrap value. Driven high enough, interest rates can thus destroy capital values. And capital values is what capitalism is all about.

This phenomena became a fright for banks. Under the United States fractional banking reserve system, where banks are permitted to hold as little as 12% in reserve for every $1 on deposit, banks can easily become as big a leveraged operator as any casino. In this example, they can lend eight times their liquid reserves. When the high rates arrive, this destroys the value of the reserve collateral, and they not only lose others' money but their own capital as well.

So, the fatal flaw in the value of capital was compound interest at high rates. It literally tore the capitalistic system apart.

ZERO YIELDS

In the late 1980s, everyone was scrambling to get a high yield on his investment, but in public discussions another flaw in the mathematical process of yields emerged was ignored. That was the yield when calculated after inflation and taxes. This was known as the "real" yield. For example, in late 1989 the yield on a three month U.S. Treasury Bill was 7.91%, but after taxes and inflation it was 0%. (Federal income taxes averaged 28%, and State taxes 5%, and with inflation at that time calculated at 6%, the yield, when they were factored in, was 0%.) Only if Treasury Bill yield rates rose to 9% would the yield be positive. This was one of the main reasons foreigners were lending to America and buying Treasury debt, because they were not subject to taxes on interest they earned. But for the American public in general, the differences between real and nominal rates of interest was poorly understood.

But although the public was oblivious in real and nominal rates of return, they were fully informed on the topic of the pursuit of money. That was all most people thought about most of the time, it seemed. They ran furiously to catch up, they used credit cards and paid 20% interest on those loans, and thought this was perfectly all right. After all, everyone else was doing it, too. Historically, they were in tune with the times. Since, in past history, as societies matured they changed their focus to the material aspect of life, money and greed ruled them as well.

That this life style was all froth, bubbles, and all bound to end was ignored, as it had been in other societies again and again in the past.

Why, then, after over 500 years should the capitalistic system—the one devoted and dedicated to capital—fall apart? It was a system that used and abused credit and did this at high rates of interest. The exponential function was not understood. All through history excessive debt creation has precipitated national crises and now was no different from other historical times.

It is simply astonishing that while the pendulum of history was swinging away from the past good times and headed towards our present bad times, that the process was not revealed in the media, or by the experts. But, experts all through history had been similarly trapped.

The basic trends were also global, meaning the entire industrial world would be impacted at the same time and at the speed of light since this is how rapidly computer monies are transferred. This insured that global breakdown would happen fast—overnight our lives would be transformed dramatically.

AN EARLY BEGINNING

The Savings and Loan crisis in America was an early sign of a growing cancer in the American financial system. By the time it reached the spotlight, a monster crisis had emerged, not a baby. It started out as a $20 billion threat, and finalized as over $400 billion of potential threats. There were only two ways of dealing with the problem back in 1989: 1) liquidate the thrifts, or 2) merge one weak institution with a stronger one. The second route was chosen because the federal government did not have the necessary resources to do the first.

To hide financial weakness, the solution was to form a new bailout agency known às the Resolution Trust Corporation. It was supposed to deal with over $300 billion of insolvent thrifts' assets that were straightforward mortgages—most of which had turned bad. It was estimated that $100 billion plus were bad and non-performing. This meant that the Resolution Trust Corporation would have to sell over $300 billion of good assets. But the total of mortgage backed securities sold in 1988 was only $167 billion, so if that agency were to sell $300 billion, that would mean expanding the market by $60 billion for five years.

By October 1989 the U.S. Treasury had to sell $650 billion in Treasury obligations, rolling them over this was called, one debt taking the place of the other. In 1988, the Treasury sold $888 billion in Treasury Bills, and most of this was financed by retiring earlier issues (roll over). Only $25 billion was net new money.

Since the U.S. Treasury was the world's biggest debtor, it also raised $109 billion in bonds with a maturity of over five years, of which only $59 billion was net new borrowing. So, by comparison, the $60 billion which the Resolution Agency needed equalled the Treasury's annual borrowing needs in over-five-year monies.

This meant that the ability of the Government to fund its debts in the financial market was becoming increasingly strained. This portended great danger for all Americans because:

1) Debt levels were already astronomically high and bearing interest at high rates. It had been estimated that if the debt continued to grow at past growth rates, and interest rates did not come down, that within ten years (1997) all of the Gross National Product in America would have to be used just to pay

interest on this debt—the exponential function at work.

2) Growing weaknesses in funding FDIC insurance, among other agencies in dire needs of new funds, threatened the solvency of the U.S. Treasury. This was because the only way it could raise funds was to borrow the funds. And this meant that it would be necessary to tap the entire savings of the nation either voluntarily or forcibly to get funds, precipitating a crisis.

But, when this string runs out, where will the funds come from for more financing?

Since debts are always paid by either debtor or the creditor, the Government faced a solvency problem—literally going broke.

MONEY ACCELERATION

The processes of funding move more quickly with computer money, so the threat of a crisis of solvency could happen much faster than any other major crisis in past U.S. history.

ENORMOUS RISK

Despite this ongoing and growing dilemma, there was no emergence of "crisis concern" among the public. In fact, in an article on this "new fiscal game," the *Wall Street Journal* on August 7, 1989 reported that among other provisions of the Savings and Loan rescue bill was one to create a new sticker to go on the doors of banks to announce that, from now on, the deposit insurance was backed by the "full faith and credit" of the United States Government.

The "full faith and credit" backing meant that the Government pledged to pay depositor's balances with funds derived from the taxpayer. But taxpayers themselves in 1989 were so heavily indebted that they could not tolerate higher taxes, because if they paid them, then they could not pay their own debts. This would create another crisis in the private sector's debt holdings of over $9 trillion. An absolute Catch 22 was in the making.

On that same subject, the *Los Angeles Times* reported August 10, 1989, "The Resolution Trust Corporation will become the largest owner and manager of real estate in the history of the world." One expert reported, "If you sold $10 million of real estate each day seven days a week, and did this for a year, with no time off, it would take 28 years to sell $100 billion, and the potential was $400 billion. How fruitless this endeavor!

THE ENORMOUS GROWTH OF FINANCIAL RISK

In the transformation from industry to money for profit, it became necessary for money dealers to constantly expand the financial instruments they dealt with, of course, to make more money. The Federal Reserve Board Chairman Alan Greenspan, in a report to Congress on June 14, 1989, commented on this phenomena by noting that "purchases and sales of U.S. Treasury Notes and Bonds, which surpassed $3 trillion on a gross basis in 1988, were up from $100 million to $100 billion a decade earlier." He referred to this as an "unbundling of financial risk." He was so bold as to continue, "the welfare of people in the United States and abroad becomes more dependent on the per-formance of external economies and exchange market (financial) developments."

Thus, the welfare of all Americans now hinged on financial market activity. And on high risk to boot. It is no wonder that we now must root through the ashes to survive. The forces that made this an imperative had been at work for years, but unless you were participating in this game, you were unaware of it. Actually, most Americans were too busy trying to make ends meet. They left the matter of their financial futures in the hands of others in government, on Wall Street and in their local bank or thrift manager's hands.

So, the historical circle has been closed again. Brooks Adams argued that over time societies become civilized, and this brings in its wake materialism, greed, and the pursuit of money.[1] Then debt loads accumulated in this growth simply fall of their own weight, and society starts anew, almost at a barbarian (hard times) plateau where fear then rules.

This is an ancient historical cycle and gives lie to the deeply imbedded American notion that "things will always get better." We all know now that this was not perpetually true. They do for one generation, perhaps two, then tough times bring us out of our sleep and back to the real world where we start to work again and where old verities such as truth emerge again…. Without basic values we perish. We must preserve our national integrity and all that goes with it. It is a shame that it is only when we are plunged into difficult times that we realize this.

THE SUPREMACY OF THE PURSUIT OF MONEY

Our love affair with money has done us all in, and it has left us more impoverished than Americans were in any other Depression on record. The $12 trillion in domestic debts being liquidated have created unusual problems at every level of our lives.

THE FOLLY OF DEBT MONEY

We are finding out that it is now quite possible that our Federal Government might become insolvent and declare bankruptcy. Why?

Our economy was built on the quicksand of debt-money. Money was created by borrowing and one of the main borrowers was the federal government. They did not print paper money as so many believed; they borrowed money to finance their activities. The problem with this was as the pace of their borrowing accelerated, it reached the point where their borrowing was creating new interest payments on old interest payments at rates of growth much faster than the growth of any of the components of the GNP (where wealth was created), so this process was one where, finally, more debt was simply breeding more bad debt. Proof? We had $12 trillion in domestic debt and just $4 trillion GNP to repay the debt, so we were broke as a nation. Financial doomsday, long predicted, had arrived.

In America and in the industrial world we face, unusually in all of economic history, the very real chance that the industrial era might be ending. Why should a society that has produced such a high standard of living for so many people for almost three hundred years be in trouble now?

There are a variety of reasons, but the three principal ones are:

1) The inability to service debts and control debt growth since debt is the lifeblood of advanced capitalistic societies.
2) The destruction of the environment by industry and the public.
3) The institutions that support the capitalistic structure are failing. If they totally stop working, the system then will fail because its props are gone.

There are other reasons, of course, including: too high migration into America; the moral breakdown of our society; the coming collapse of our national infrastructure which will grind the system to a halt by itself as our bridges, roads and sewers, water and other systems fail, etc.

THE CURRENT DEBT PROBLEM

1) The extension of credit has brought many good things to Americans, but the overextension and abuse of bank credit will bring in its wake a financial disaster into the

lives of most Americans. Why must this be?

The Wall Street Journal surveyed over 40 mainstream economists to get their predictions for 1990.[2] Their average guess was that the Gross National Product would grow about 2% during 1990 and long-term bond yields would average 8%.

Assume they are correct. What is so wrong? If Gross National Product grows at 2% compounded, this amount doubles in 36 years. The long-term bonds at an 8% rate, compounded, doubles in 9 years. Since our money is debt-money, the credit dollars double four times faster than the economic growth (that pays it back) in the 36 year time span. Therefore, debts in 36 years will be four times larger than the wealth that is supposed to pay the debts and back. And that is what is basically wrong with the finances of capitalism. We cannot repay our debts in the long run.

The debt burden must grow steadily to provide the funds for economic growth and then become so large as to become unsustainable. This always results in debt default or repudiation—but the debts cannot be paid. And, too bad for our society, they are repaid in hard times.

Can't we, then, go back to the old days of saving before we spend? Not unless we first go through the travail of debt liquidation and hard times which is what we may be starting to do now. Won't the end of this trouble mean that we will revert to our old American habits of thrift and saving? We could, of course, but if we did then our economic growth would be crippled because it is leveraged debt that accelerates economic growth as we have learned to our dismay, and the additional disappearance of our free Mother Lode resources, as described in this book, further insures economic growth will be ever-so-slow from now on.

Leveraged debt was a gas chamber for our society, but our major banks did not think so—they went to great pains to make leveraged loans. Citibank ran an ad in which they stated, "At Citibank, we believe financing can help breathe new life into a company, giving it the ability to more successfully compete in today's global marketplace."[3] At that time of this ad some of the great leveraged corporations were heading for the financial graveyard—Campeau, Drexel-Burnham, Integrated Resources and more debtors would surely follow.

So, the death of leveraged debt plus the vanishing free lunch enjoyed in the Mother Lode together guarantee a dramatic change in our economic system...and probably in our lives from now on.

2. The destruction of the environment must end, and it will. In the fast-paced life of the 1980s we consumed furiously and ignored the hidden costs of this lifestyle. We threw our garbage away, for example, thinking someone else would take care of it. They did, but the long-term consequences were perilous as in California for example, it was estimated that by 1995 all the landfills, where garbage is dumped, would be filled by the year 2000.[4]

You cannot produce material goods endlessly, as we have, without incurring soaring hidden costs. In the early stages, the costs are ignored, but they do not go away and add up rapidly. In one study it was estimated that if we cannot build an environmentally sustainable society by 2030, environmental deterioration and economic decline would feed on each other causing social structures to disintegrate.[5]

The study went on to observe that our never-ending reliance on fossil fuels, natural gas and oil, will cause "catastrophic changes in climate." This would require a massive shift to solar power for water heating, as the Japanese have done. As we move away from coal-fired and oil-fired power plants there will be a much smaller role for the automobile, reducing their numbers and role significantly within forty years. The production and use of cars makes up close to 3% of our Gross National Product, so the cutback here would be devastating for our economic growth. This, of course, dispels growing fears that by 2000, or thereabouts, we will have the OPEC nations at our throats again as they were in 1974.

The study continued that for the human race to hold its own, the next 40 years must see an abandonment of fossil fuels, a downturn in birth rates, an end to forest and farmland destruction and a trejection of the "throw-away society." All of these items comprise the center of our old capitalistic system. If they cannot be accomplished, then the capitalistic system must end since all of these items account for much of its growth and continuance. And, the two are totally incompatible.

3. During the 1980s the American public saw a rapid decline in many of capitalism's institutions. Every form of society needs its own institutions to keep the system running. Their health is crucial. When they fail, the system's troubles start in earnest.

Education: The decline in education to everyone. Advanced degrees all through history have been for the few, not the many, and this is not an elitist view. It is a reality. But in an effort to expand a small education base to take care of a vast surge in students the education standards necessarily fell. And this decline spread down to the lowest grades. Pretty soon all of the high school students were dropping out, and the students that graduated were functionally illiterate, etc. Where will the people come from to run the economic machine tomorrow if the recent students cannot read, write, or spell?

Health Care: Almost forty million Americans have no health care, no insurance-nothing. The Los Angeles

Times on February 3, 1990, ran a poll on this topic and a majority favored nationalized medicine. We all remember the day when a doctor would ask us "Where does it hurt?" Today a doctor asks "Do you have insurance?" That is a sample of the change we have had in our health care and our perception of it over the years. Our hospitals are too full, our emergency centers are shutting down, no young woman wants to learn to be a nurse. Something is very wrong, and must be changed.

Legal System: Our courts are jammed, our prisons are overflowing, crime is rampant, we do not have enough police. All of these signs are similar to the breakdown of the legal system in Rome in its decline, and our legal system was adapted from theirs. We love "justice" but it is hard to find. And if we don't find it, it will complicate our turnaround tomorrow much longer.

Political System: Most Americans gave up voting a long time ago. We truly have a form of government that is not at all representative. Our politicians have been transformed into professionals who are in office far too long and who do not represent their constituents any longer. Thus, to tout the virtues of "democracy" is to talk about a form of political organization that no longer exists.

The Military: We have spent literally trillions on our military forces, and they do not work. Every time they are used in combat, they display ineptness. We have billions of dollars of military equipment rusting away, or stored in warehouses never to be used. We must transform this nightmare organization before it transforms us for good.

The Corporations: Our corporations have been transformed from liquid and creative organizations to debt loaded groups that create few new products, buy technology to cut labor costs, and do not take care of the workers as they did even in the days of the Robber Barons, long ago.

Our Financial System: This is now the lifeblood of our society and it is in total disarray. It will be, must be, revamped totally. An old historical saying goes that if you debauch your money, you debauch your society. We have learned the truth of that wisdom.

What, then is still good about our society? First and foremost, the indominitable spirit of the American people. They are good, honest and fair; they work hard, and they have a God-driven spirit that will protect them and guide them in restoring our system. However, our system tomorrow will not be restored under the old industrial concept that "bigger is better," on the accumulation of capital, on flawed inheritance laws, on compound interest—on those old and failed ideas of capitalism.

No, our society will be restructured on a new plateau: on the growth of small business which is a true capitalism, with the reemergence of the entrepreneur; on native inventiveness; on all of the natural attributes that made America a great country. All of these verities, morals and wisdoms of the past will return, but only after we go through the economic fire of a dramatically slowed down economy with losses of jobs and incomes. The economics of societies through history is like that—it is no bed of roses.

LOOKING BACK: INFLATION, DEFLATION?

Inflation by 1990 was a historical artifact. No one who is reading this book will ever see inflation again in their lifetime. Our society and, in fact, the entire world is in the early stages of a very long period of deflation that is gradually growing into the worst depression in U.S. history. Over the last 700 years, there have been three periods of extreme deflation. This is the fourth, and will prove to be by far the worst such period.

Deflation is underway and accelerating, and this has been going on since 1973. Deflation is a period of economic contraction. Real prices and wages have fallen—contracted—about 18 percent since 1973. But this deflation will include not only falling prices and falling wages, but total economic collapse, as well.

If a worker has less to spend, he spends less. And if he becomes unemployed, his spending decreases just to absolute necessity. This spending decrease will continue and eventually feed through the entire economy.

The days of American growth and material well-being are gone. It will seem like forever before they return—if they ever do.

The first time that it will be apparent to the average man that anything is wrong will be, perhaps, after a collapse in the world's stock markets. After stocks fall steeply, companies will be desperately searching for any source of liquidity to pay off debt—cutting costs, firing workers, saving, not spending.

A severe credit contraction—actually a credit collapse—will then develop as sources of credit dry up. Interest rates will soar, with short-term rates climbing as high as 40 percent. We will see, briefly, by far the highest interest rates in American history, and it will literally destroy business as we know it.

As the collapse occurs, we will then face a huge money panic. The Dow index in inflation-adjusted terms will end up where it was in 1933, when it fell as low as 41. We could have a bank holiday. If so, the money supply will then vanish and the stock and commodity exchanges will also close. We may have to do without public utilities, fire protection, police protection and the like if the collapse is as serious as I anticipate. As they do in every really severe crisis, gold and silver prices will soar. Gold prices will rise to $2,000 an ounce and silver to more than $100 an ounce. However, these prices may not stay high for a long period. Who knows?

The real estate crash that has already been experienced in several parts of the country will spread all over America. In most areas of the country, all types of real estate—commercial and residential—will be selling for as low as ten cents per dollar in terms of today's prices. In some areas of the country, it will fall to one cent on the dollar.

Don't think this won't happen. It has happened before, and it will happen again. In 1832, houses selling for $15,000 in Chicago collapsed in value to less than $100 in one year. More recently, in the late 1920s, real estate on the southern Florida coast fell 99 percent. Where the biggest boom in real estate prices are occurring right now—Southern California—is where the biggest collapse is going to occur.

The government will be under extraordinary pressure when that happens, and the only way it can save property from truly mass foreclosure is to place a moratorium on mortgage payments until real estate values are written down to more realistic levels. Of course, this means that just about every savings and loan institution in the country and many banks will be broke. No, the U.S. government is not about to step in and save the banks. They'd face an armed insurrection first.

No one knows exactly when these events will occur. It could begin in a few weeks or months, or a few years. The timing is *not* knowable. The Bible says that *"men are trapped when bad times suddenly come."* The situation described will develop in a matter of months.

The idea of credit contracting is not well understood. One analogy most people understand was in the price of oil. When oil prices fell a few years ago, most people didn't understand that oil is financed like everything else. So, when oil prices fell, the financing for oil exploration and recovery collapsed as well.

Companies in the oil business whose cash flows had already been reduced by the oil price collapse could no longer service the interest on their debt. In turn, they could not obtain the financing they needed to see them through the crisis since they had no way to pay off the previous ones. This in turn led to even greater restriction in the oil company's cash flows as banks called in the loans they had already extended. A vicious cycle of default/debt contraction was created.

Now, what happened to the oil industry is now happening to the entire economy. The growth of credit from 1945-1980 has gone into reverse. Despite the best efforts of the Federal Reserve and other government agencies, there's no way anyone can increase the amount of credit in the economy at a time when it will be most desperately needed.

I think that the future is always a consequence of events that have occurred in the past. Our future will be dictated primarily because of the liquidation of the enormous debts that we have acquired. In the United States alone, we have $14 trillion in domestic debts.

The key to the problem of debt in our society is *compound interest*. Compound interest means that enormous amounts of interest must be paid on any type of debt. For instance, just to service the $14 trillion domestic debt, over $1.4 trillion in interest must be paid each year. This insures the debt principal cannot be repaid. Unfortunately, most mainstream economists ignored the problem of compound interest, assuming the debt problem will somehow just go away.

About twenty percent of domestic debt is federal debt and the remaining eighty percent is private debt. While the debt that everyone worries about is the federal debt, the really worrisome debt is the $10 trillion private debt. It is this enormous debt that will sink us.

The $10 trillion in private debt is much more dangerous than public debt because it is supported by the thinnest of resources. The private sector is by far the largest source of credit creation, not the government or the Federal Reserve. This private credit has been granted on extremely questionable terms. It is far too weak to withstand a shock.

Corporations are in debt beyond belief. A typical example was Campeau, which took on so much debt that 80 percent of their income was required to service it. And this debt load, while hugely excessive, is about average for U.S. corporations. Campeau's fortunes were reversed when slow retail sales reduced cash flows—making debt service difficult. The company had to declare bankruptcy to escape this debt load, and most of its employees will lose their jobs.

In a microcosm, this is what happened to the American corporation. The $4.0 trillion in private corporate debt will unravel, just like it did at Campeau. We've created a financial nuclear bomb that is exploding and will infest every nook and cranny of the economy—not just in the United States, but worldwide.

The remaining $6.0 trillion of private debt is consumer debt. Consumers are, for the most part, dependent on other people for their incomes. If they lose their job, their debts don't get paid. The same cycle of debt contraction that happened in the oil industry starts.

No economy can be so productive that it can generate enough wealth to pay off a huge percentage of its capacity in debt service. The expense of paying interest on huge debts is counted now as "part of doing business." In fact, businesses have to raise prices because their interest payments are so large that they have no choice. This looks like inflation, but it isn't. One trillion four hundred million dollars in interest payments translates to about a 4 percent increase in prices annually. Prices have to rise this much each year by simply to pay interest on the outstanding $1.4 trillion in debt.

When prices are adjusted for this *debt inflation,* we find that prices are actually falling like a rock in real terms. In fact, one authority on this subject, Professor Margrit Kennedy, in Steyerberg, Germany, has calculated that one-half the price of anything we buy represents past or current interest expenses.

Another giant-sized problem is that much of the privately-held debt is highly-leveraged, particularly in real estate. Leverage works both ways: when prices are rising, it's wonderful, but when they're falling, you can lose very quickly. I estimate current commercial real estate market losses in today's economy to be about $800 million.

Banks now are holding on to thousands of worthless commercial mortgages and are unwilling to admit this loss. But it exists, nonetheless, and is worst in the oil patch states. In addition, there is an additional $4 trillion in outstanding residential mortgage debt that is highly leveraged. When the real estate market crashes, most of this credit will be gone forever.

The financial sector in America is *far larger* than the industrial sector—about three times as large. And finance is where the most serious problems are. When the financial sector slumps, so goes the rest of America.

The problem is debt, which starts a destructive cycle of compound interest payments which entail the taking on of more debt. After the crash, I expect we will evolve into a society where debts are resolved in ways that don't involve the payment of interest. Like the Moslem religion, we may actually view charging interest as a blasphemy.

The government is totally helpless to stop the breakdown. It can do nothing to reflate the economy once the crash happens.

No governmental agency could stop the crash in October 19, 1987 in the stock market. And this was only a small sign of what is ahead. The Federal Reserve can't prevent interest rates from going up because it does not really control credit. The Fed can only create reserves, not actually make loans. If a bank needs credit, it can go onto the Eurobond market in a few milliseconds electronically and borrow. The Fed's "reserve requirements" today mean next to nothing when it comes to influencing interest rates. Finally, the assets of a pair of large U.S. Banks such as Citibank and Chase Manhattan are larger than the reserves of the Federal Reserve.

The supply of money tends to contract when the rate of spending declines. That only makes sense—an unemployed man isn't terribly creditworthy. This actually intensifies the depression, and is precisely what happened during the Great Depression of the 1930s.

We need, of course, some entity to actually increase the money supply when a depression hits instead of allowing it to contract. but human nature being what it is, no one wants to be responsible for sending "good money after bad." It is only human nature for a credit contraction to accompany and intensify a depression.

Various government "bailout programs" to take effect during the truly catastrophic depression will be futile. The various programs that supposedly will protect your bank accounts, will not.

The Federal Insurance Deposit Corporation, which supposedly insures bank deposits, is not better off. The FDIC has less than .08 cents on hand to insure every dollar that it is supposed to insure. Moreover, $11 billion of the $18 billion that the FDIC is supposed to have has already been loaned out to busted banks and lost forever.

Nor will reinflation work. If the government spends money to reinflate the economy, what really happens? If the government lends money to a farmer to help him pay off his bank, the farmer isn't really any better off. His debt has only been transferred from the bank to the government. Of course, the government can still write off the debt, but the government, contrary to popular opinion, can no more create money out of thin air than can the banks. The only thing the government can do is trade money from one capital account to another. It can do nothing to end the depression by "re-inflating" the economy.

Most economists don't understand how the economy has changed due to the massive debts that have been incurred. They focus on traditional problems like inflation and ignore new ones such as an $14 trillion domestic debt.

Until the private sector has once again regains the confidence to both lend and spend, our entire credit system will be paralyzed. Our nation will be like Mexico is today, where loans are made for 150 percent interest if you qualify—which is almost impossible. Very few people will either ask for, or be granted, credit until confidence returns.

The public has no control over the forces of deflation. They are helpless. People do have control over their own psychological outlook, but once you lose your job and your credit-worthiness, your positive attitude will evaporate! You will be filled with fear, particularly if you haven't prepared in advance for hard times. The average person, if he simply uses his own good sense and looks around him to see what is happening in this country, will come to the same conclusions that I have. Even if I'm only half right, we are headed for a disaster. People need to take appropriate steps to prepare.

Electronic technology and satellite communications make today's economy more susceptible to depressions. In the Great Depression, everything that could have gone wrong, did go wrong. In this depression, everything will still go wrong—but do so at the speed of light. Everyone knows instantly when the first occurrence of a problem is and takes instant steps to hedge it. This is why there will be no bank lines when the next depression hits—the big corporations and foreign depositors that constantly monitor the markets will take their money out first, and there's no way the government will be able to guarantee the small depositor the return of his deposits.

It seems to me electronics have influenced us by focusing our attention on the trivial. Instead of looking at long-term debt, we look at today's trade deficit. A corporation lives for its quarterly earnings, not its long-term competitive stance. None of these short-term trends are significant. For instance, the trade data is always revised a few days after the initial announcement. Yet the markets almost always react to the initial announcement, and rarely the correction.

A repudiation by the government on its debts is possible—it could happen. This would then be a time to head for the hills, because it would be followed by a total breakdown in society and the start of a new "dark age" in American history.

There has been much written in the past 10 years about a coming societal change. I think signs abound that the industrial era, just 300 years old, may be now drawing to a close. Few of our institutions work well anymore. The financial system is in shambles, the welfare system does not work the prisons are overflowing and rampant with riots, and the political forces in Washington are paralyzed and unable to act, and so on.

The one thing to prepare for in the future is the future.

HOW WILL THE PUBLIC REACT TO THE COMING CRISIS?

Sometime about 20 years ago, America turned from a structured, orderly, relatively stable society into one run by power blocs, each with a narrow focus on its own interest. During that period the U.S. economy also lost much of its dynamism.

From a review of the last 60 years, one startling contrast emerges. That is the difference in the way Americans responded during the first 10 years of the half-century compared with the response in the 1960s and 1970s. In the 1930s, the public demonstrated exemplary patience despite considerable suffering from the abysmal economic conditions. Unemployment, hunger, cold, and death notwithstanding, there were no riots, revolts or coups d'etat.

No such patience was shown in the 1960s and 1970s. They were a time of riots and civil disobedience, of refusal to serve in the military. The government, instead of being rejected, became suspect. This disillusionment has not been dispelled even now.

From the years of the 1930s, the years of crisis, war, and drama, the U.S. has changed from a simple society—principally exploiting the natural resources of a heavily endowed continent—into a complex urban society where, for many years, America dominated the world. Back in 1929 American business still often reflected the personality of the founding entrepreneurs—Ford, Rockefeller, etc.—whose aim was not only to make money but also to build an empire that would immortalize the founder's name. By now most of these businesses had developed into giant impersonal multinationals, run by professional managers whose focus was short term, mainly on earnings per share. Distrust of these corporations grew and coincided with a build up of environmental and transportation problems that threatened to over-whelm society.

WHAT ABOUT THE FUTURE?

So, just as 1929 was a watershed year, 1990 is also one of crisis and change. By 2029 people will have recognized that now marked the end of industrial society as we have defined it. The tendency to mass operations, which built the world economy to today's high levels, has peaked.

The businesses that will prosper tomorrow will be the small, cottage-industry type, a form of true capitalism, who will apply individual creativity to the emerging problems. There will be no more standardizing of society and its components as we now see around us.

As the industrial society goes, so will mass production, mass marketing, and mass media. The industrial society of our past was based on cheap fossil fuels, the level of technology we attained, mass distribution and transportation, mass education, the multinational corporation, the mass media, and most of all on the notion of the "marketplace." Further, a vital part was the concentration of political power in Washington, D.C., plus the growing close relationship between big business and big government.

These dependencies will be gone and are, in fact, leaving. Right now steel, auto, railroad-equipment, machinery, appliance, textile, shoe, and apparel industries are moving to producers outside America because American corporations, for many reasons, are unable or unwilling to compete, or have so burdened themselves with debts as to be corpses themselves.

We will not turn into a society where we take in each other's laundry. We will, as mass production wanes, turn into a society where business is conducted on a small scale, in small communities away from cities, and where we walk to work instead of needing a car to get there. We will more resemble America before the turn of the century than America in 1988.

The extraordinary crisis now in the making will change the way most of us think about a lot of things, including medicine, transport, lawyers, accountants, and education. These institutions and others were formed around (and served) the capitalistic mode of society. But when the capitalistic mode of society dies, so will their form, and they will emerge very different in order to cope with the debris of capitalism, now gone.

THE ILLUSION OF PROSPERITY IS GONE

We might well recognize that all of our good times, all of our growth, and all of our prosperity since the 1930s was bought on credit. None of it was paid for, and the debts just kept growing. Now they are at levels unprecedented in all economic history going back to the beginning.

WILL THE DEBTS BE REPAID?

First and foremost are Uncle Sam's debts since they directly and indirectly impinge on us all.

Right now those debts are headed for trouble. Many other formidable institutions are nearing the debt brink: banks, thrifts, oilmen, farmers, and so on.

Where will Uncle Sam get the funds to pay interest on its own full faith and credit debt, T-bills, notes, bonds, GNMAEs, and savings bonds?

Also, since U.S. Treasury Bonds are collateral for our paper money (Federal Reserve Notes), paper money will have no value if the Treasury Bonds are defaulted. Nor will anything else, for that matter.

How could the government pay interest on its own debt? The Federal Reserve could borrow the funds, pay for them by credits at Treasury accounts, and the Treasury could use these credit proceeds to send interest due to owners of government debt.

But, by definition, this extra borrowing is tantamount to "watering down" Uncle Sam's creditworthiness, making the debt instruments worth less as it accelerated. This will finally lead to foreigners selling their own U.S. debts holdings, destroying our bond markets, banks, and thrifts in the process, as they withdraw their vast holdings. Uncle Sam would then be much like a Latin debtor: insolvent.

What can the government do? Perhaps redefine debt repayment terms, changing 90-day Treasury Bills into 30-year bonds—delaying interest payments—*anything to survive.*

What's wrong with that? Public confidence could vanish. The public, already pressed by the hard times, may tend towards anarchy. This could lead to a revolt and an upheaval of our entire political system. It could happen.

CHAPTER THIRTEEN

REFERENCES

1. Brooks Adams.

2. *Wall Street Journal*, January 2, 1990.

3. *Wall Street Journal*, February 8, 1990.

4. *Los Angeles Times,* February 11, 1990, p. 40.

5. *State of the World 1990.*

CHAPTER FOURTEEN

THE GOOD NEWS CHAPTER

The argument in this book is fairly straightforward: the industrial era may be drawing to a close; America's economic and financial systems are overdue for an epic correction and transformation; our standard of living will fall as we go through a prolonged period of hard times. I based the general argument on four observations:

1) Back in the 1930s a host of government "safety nets" were invented and implemented. Their purpose was to prevent another deflationary depression. Now, however, the risks that the government was supposed to insure, guarantee, support, fund, etc., are now the main means by which the deflationary depression will happen and intensify, as I have written.

2) How long does it take with compound interest for an accumulated debt burden to weight on the solvency of the federal government? That time is near, I believe— perhaps before the end of this decade. No one can know precisely this soon.

3) Since interest cost compounds much faster than national wealth output, which provides the only means to repay, it is only a question of time until it will prove to be impossible for the financial and economic systems in America to avoid a giant-sized breakdown with the federal

government leading the way—"the American bank of last resort" failing.

4) The burden of total interest costs rises as more of the total credits created in our society are diverted to pay the compounding interest bill. In addition, since continued new extension of credit must always now fall below the total growing cost of compound interest costs, the entire economic system is forced to liquidate its debts to restore solvency.

YOUR POSITION

As a reader, up until now you will fall into one of two groups: 1) you totally disbelieve the argument, and believe in your heart of hearts that the American system will somehow muddle through, like England has done since the 1930s, or 2) you are inclined to think the argument has a ring of truth and basic merit. If you are in this group, there are things you can do now to preserve your self and your family from utter chaos, and keep afloat financially simultaneously as the ship of state sinks.

During a period like our past in America since 1945, the creditor has occupied an undeniably comfortable position. And this holds true in times past in America when we had stable production and the storing of wealth. If this were not true, there would be no creditors. But the creditor class has never been permitted too much happiness. That would be against nature. The law of compensation requires that for every sleepless night passed by a debtor there should be a nightmare suffered by a creditor. It may not be the same night. It may be long deferred. Broadly, it seems unlikely that both creditors and debtors can be happy at the same time: though it was quite possible, during the modern debt manipulation in America during the 1980s, and under the influence of such vast federal borrowing which created an economic laughing-gas which was pumped upon this country and the world from 1980 to 1989, and both may make outcries of anesthetic a pleasure. As we are now emerging from this deep debt sleep, the two classes will find their interests dissimilar. Upon this discovery, the debtor applies to the politician; the creditor to the majesty of the law. Then a race develops to see whether the politician can change the laws or the laws resist the politician.

The creditor is always vulnerable and, finally, it always works that the creditor gets what he can, as we are now seeing. In our modern banker-economy, when the lending is mainly by them, and the risks are spread, defaults are far more numerous, but less burdensome on an individual creditor. He then belongs to a sort of guild, with some political as well as legal power and influence. His eggs are not in the same basket. There are methods of enforcing payment, or of exacting penalties, but the early stages of the downturn do not bring him into personal disrepute. As the breakdown consumes everyone, however, the banker then emerges as the scapegoat. He is reviled and the public is ready to do him in.

We have forgotten one economic truth: the creditor is under a moral obligation and an economic obligation not to lend unconscionably. What should have mattered most is that the creditor did not incur a credit position without care, diligence and a conviction of wisdom and rightness of the loan. Reckless lending is taboo and Turgot warned in his Formation et Distribution de Richesses" three centuries ago. "The lender cares about two things only: the interest he is to receive, and the safety of his capital. He does not trouble himself about the use the borrower will make of it, anymore than the merchant concerns himself with the use his purchaser will make of the commodities he sells him." This idea no longer bears inspection. It was, instead, the frivolous and reckless modern lending policies which was responsible for all of the broken contracts we have seen in America in recent years and, cumulatively, which has now brought our economy to receivership.

During most of 1989 and into 1990, I was a guest on many radio talk shows all over America discussing the contents of my book, *How To Profit From the Next Great Depression.* In that book, I recommended that people invest their surplus funds in 90-Day U.S. Treasury Bills or (EE) Savings Bonds. As time went on, more and more people questioned that wisdom with this recurring question, "Why should I invest in Treasury Debts if the government's debts are as huge as they are? Isn't that risky?"

The fact that public opinion was homed in on that truth was a far cry from the accepted truths on Wall Street and in the banking industry, who were rushing to put the public's funds into Treasury Debt instruments. It merely revealed that those at the short end of the income stream were, as always, intuitively ahead of the accepted investing wisdom.

It will be argued by most experts that the government debt problems can, over time, be settled outside of default. But the lessons in other countries historically is that this cannot be done. Individuals, however, by taking certain precautions now can protect their own future and destinies to a large degree.

It is certainly not my intent to fulminate like an Old Testament prophet against the ignorance, prejudice, indifference, bureaucratic inertia and ineptitude that may be leading us to a national debt crisis. After all, the public wants good times forever, and politicians, to stay in office, had better deliver them. Their method of accomplishing this in our economy is to borrow and spend and to issue more debt than we will ever have the ability to repay. The awesome and unrelenting power of compound interest has, from the beginning, staggered and then sunk borrowers, and we may rediscover this ancient truism in our time.

THE LOST DECADE

It is not another millennium dirge to suggest that the 1990s may prove to be the Lost Decade for Americans just as the 1980s was the Lost Decade for the Latin nations. It was there, in the Third World, in bondage and suffering under monumental debts, where living standards had plunged from 1980 to 1990 as an

estimated $204 billion flowed out of the region, mostly to ser-
vice a collective debt of over $430 billion.[1] The gross national
product in most of those nations shrank in the 1980s together
with real wages, imposing savage financial strains on those poor
peoples as they tried to pay back rich lenders.

The middle to the end of the 1990s may prove to be a part of
the Lost Decade for most of us in America as our own government
tries maybe fruitlessly to service its own mammoth debts—and
tries to do this in hard times—during a crippling depression,
when the private sector itself is on the financial ropes, and an
extraordinary shortage of credit becomes the new reality.

But most Americans may not want to believe this chain of
events because hope has always sprung eternal in the American
psyche. And their deep-seated beliefs will be reinforced by the
old guard, who will promise endlessly that the federal debt riddle
is manageable, really nothing at all, and even falsely suggest that
the Federal Reserve will ride to the rescue—not realizing that
this idea will abort at birth. They will probably also be furious at
the suggestion that there might be federal fiscal problems that
can no longer be resolved in the workings of the old system—
that the "borrow and spend" era is gone forever.

But beyond the Federal debt bomb lies our own unbelievable
consumer debt problems, estimated to be $4.3 trillion[2] coupled
with corporate and city and state deficits, aggregating over $9
trillion. Since most of us are caught in our own personal debt
traps, we have personal knowledge and experience of just how
difficult it is to dig your way out of debt with high rates of
interest which compounds while we sleep. So, our fears for
Uncle Sam's debts are realistic.

THE END OF ECONOMIC GROWTH

The end of material progress may well be at hand. If so, this
could present enormous psychological problems for all of us
since our national religion has been in growth, motherhood,

apple pie, rising incomes, and the widespread belief that things will always get better.

Now our most deeply held national belief-systems will be put into reverse, and we will all have difficulty coping with that. Could it, in the bitter end, get as bad for us as it was for the Romanians? The *Wall Street Journal* reported on January 2, 1990:

"This is truly a classless society. Everyone is poor. Most Romanians work six days a week, and earn the equivalent of about $350 per month at the official exchange rate—worth only $30 on the black market. It takes at least three years' salary, all of it, to buy a new car. While food supplies have improved, lines for gasoline in some cities stretched for more than two miles last week. In the countryside life is more medieval than modern; some families share rooms with pigs, and horse-drawn cars are more common than cars."

If, as simple arithmetic reveals, our government is faced with the threat of debt repudiation, then obviously the wave of materialism and mindless consumption is over. One of our national delusions was that we could continue this lifestyle forever. But John Stuart Mill, English economist-philosopher, predicted over a century ago that if the Western World took the road we have in fact taken, our environment must be eventually destroyed.

He wrote, "The earth must lose that great portion of its pleasantness which it owes to things that the unlimited increase in wealth...would extirpate from it.... I sincerely hope, for the sake of posterity that future generations will be content to be stationary, long before necessity compels them to it." Mills made the inescapable point: Unlimited increases in wealth and work in a limited world is simply impossible. An economy like ours that was based on expanding needs, consumption and work had, we will find, these limits. To reverse this historic, large-scale American trend—as we are now being forced to do—will involve what the British historian E. P. Thompson called "a novel dialectic," in which we will be forced to learn what workers in the nineteenth century knew: Work and economic growth are not ends in themselves but are means to a healthy living and superior earthly and heavenly values.

Most of our investments with money, and our wealth-gathering ideas were based on the past we have lived and personally experienced. But now a totally new era is very likely nearing. Maybe, for awhile, there could be a time when we might have no organized financial markets operating for trading securities, where holdings of U.S. Treasury debt are immobilized along with other markets. Where, because of the partial settlement of $14 trillion in domestic debts (through forced liquidation and real losses), and the breakdown in federal government credit appears inescapable, the value of our dollar-denominated assets cannot be determined. Our dollar measuring rod may have vaporized. And, we could also be living in a society where this financial chaos will reign for who knows how long?

Many episodic, random events will paralyze business operations as we have known them. It will also be a period of growing social unrest because millions of Americans will be thrown out of work and have no income. Many perhaps will also lose their cars through repossession. Some will be on the verge of losing their homes, and so on. This will develop a mindset that will welcome any kind of change from the past. So, the coming social crisis will be on a larger scale than anything that has happened in America since the American Revolution.

This will be no replay of the 1930s where men sold apples on street corners. No. This will be a period of vast, national social upheaval, as the public rebels at the tragic turn of events and the radical transformations in their own lives.

Back in the 1970s when it was thought America would be in the throes of a hyperinflation, the idea of "survival techniques" resurfaced. Alas. The 1970s was the wrong time and more inflation was also the totally wrong reason. Now is that time.

Here are steps you should start taking *now*. Remember they are only temporary and designed to carry you over for a few months until social order is established again.

LAST-DITCH SURVIVAL GUIDE

With our financial world shutting down and our monies at great risk, there are important steps we can take as individuals to prevent losing the money we have worked so hard to get. They are:

1) Banks, thrifts, and credit unions will no longer be safe places to deposit your money. Draw out all of your funds and keep them at home; for now, at least $1,000 in cash in Federal Reserve Notes. Keep this cash at home since bank safe deposit boxes may not be safe anymore. As debt repudiation nears, you will want to convert this cash into gold and silver coins. By this time you should be out of "paper" representations of wealth such as Certificates of Deposit, Money Market Funds, Mutual Funds, Stocks, Bonds, etc.

   Put your remaining money resources into gold and silver coins. Believe it or not, hide these coins at home; since safe deposit boxes will no longer be safe, this is your only recourse.

   Will gold be confiscated? Probably. And this will be time for Americans to copy the French peasant who for centuries has kept gold hidden at home having learned at great cost of the treachery of government. It is said that the French peasants have more gold stored at home than the French central bank has in its coffers.

2) What about your investments in Government debt instruments—T-Bills, (EE) Savings Bonds, etc.? The signal of major trouble with government debt paper will be sharply rising interest rates (causing the prices of government debts to fall). When this happens, cash them in and buy more gold and silver coins.

3) Your real estate? You probably should have sold your home in 1989 or 1990, but if you still own in a city, rent it and move to a rural area. If you cannot leave your job,

then move your family out of the city. We must all try to get away from upcoming riots, etc., which will erupt mainly in cities.

4) Make sure you have enough clothes, toiletries and other personal necessities to tide you over the period when distribution breaks down and store shelves are empty. Include, of course, flashlights, matches and other survival-type gear.

5) Keep your car in tip-top shape. You will need it. And get a manual on how to maintain it yourself if that becomes necessary.

6) Buy a powerful radio, so you can keep in touch with what is going on.

7) There will be power outages and other communication breakdowns, including no mail deliveries for a time, telephone service being intermittent, computers and fax machines inoperative, etc.

8) Buy a generator for your home to insure you have electricity there.

9) It is not practical to try and raise enough produce for a family at home. Instead, store dried foods until food stores are full again.

10) It is only prudent to have guns at home.

In sum, plan now on having to do a lot of "surviving" wherever you live, so you will have additional ideas beyond this list of what you personally should do.

GOVERNMENT THREATS

"Modern" economic times began in the 1700s. In the almost 300 years since, every major government, regardless of political tendencies or leadership, has enacted restrictive capital regulations whenever threatened economically. France during the Revolution, Germany in the 1920s, the United States during the Civil War and in 1932, England in the 1960s, and Canada in 1989 have all in one way or another enacted laws where the public wound up footing the bill for government's economic mismanagement.

The history of America is filled with incidents of government ordering bank closures, capital confiscation and repudiation of international monetary agreements. But what makes the present time so vastly different from the past (and more dangerous) is the Everest-sized levels of debt spread throughout the land.

WATER: Have access to water away from the ongoing water supply systems which in many cities in early 1990 were in major trouble: New York City and Philadelphia are two prime examples already of major cities with ancient and leaking water systems a hundred or so years of age and badly in need of repair now. Storing water at home in jugs is only a temporary and not a satisfactory method for the long-term.

FOOD: Long-term food storage packages are available all over America. Have a supply at home together with other staples like rice and beans. Keep some canned goods in storage.

GASOLINE: Keep your car(s) filled with gasoline at all times. There will probably be breakdowns in fuel distribution because tank truck drivers could be sitting duck targets for an upset public and will refuse to drive their gasoline trucks.

ENERGY: Plan now to install a generator in your home to keep you independent of the present electric power systems.

NEIGHBORS: Start now to begin to really know your neighbors. We are all in this together and you will need help from others as they will need your help.

RURAL LIVING: Large cities will quickly become uninhabitable and centers of vast public unrest. Anarchy might also emerge quickly. So, plan now to move out of cities and beyond suburbia—which is falling apart—into the country.

Economic life tomorrow will probably trend towards jobs in small communities and not in working in large factories near cities like yesterday. Why? Small business provides jobs, new ideas, closeness to work, etc., and a chain of small businesses can make anything we want from cars to trains without the concentration of large factories and capital.

This work-relocation is just one of tomorrow's coming changes as the industrial era ends. It is just over three hundred years old, but it seems now highly unlikely that it can go on since that mode of life, among other things, destroys Nature. Nature simply will not allow that crime any longer.

For a time there will be a breakdown in law and order. There could also be dispersed anarchic episodes with every man for himself. It is only prudent to be able to protect yourself with a gun. Yes, a gun.

In this dangerous transition period from yesterday to tomorrow, travel could be restricted. Food shortages will grow as national transportation systems break down, etc. What then? Out of social disorder will come order, but who can know now how this will be restored?

The national financial breakdown will be complete and devastating, and much like the fiscal crisis in France in 1789 after which Napoleon came to power. We will also witness the end of our two-party democratic systems, and, as I have suggested, be ruled by a power figure. The move in 1989 by Eastern European countries from totalitarian control to democracy was a traditional and historical turn of events, but democracies breaking down often opt for totalitarian forms. This completes the historical circle in one nation after another over long-time spans.

A dictator could quickly restore order. And, the public will want some form of personal security restored in their lives...rapidly. We covet this security in our lives but ignore it until a crisis focuses our attention on it.

Who will fill the emerging power gap and restore order? Probably the military. In many other countries over very long historical periods, this has been the solution. In a power gap, there will be many wanting to seize control, and all sorts of zany ideas and people will emerge to try to capture the public's will. Why not, then, the military?

Can't we, somehow, go back to the old order, our old way of

living? It seems highly unlikely. After a period of social unrest, the public will demand a return of stability in their lives, and will not cling to the past power system. Order must be restored promptly lest this chaos gets out of control.

Since the American Revolution, life in America has been one of seemingly unending growth and social stability. And this has also repeated a great lesson of history. But, there has also, all through history, been times of reversal, regrouping, and total stagnation by many societies. Now is such a time for Americans.

For example in recent times, in Argentina in 1988, mail was not delivered for over a month and local transportation systems literally did not run at all. Prepare for that to happen in America sometime in the 1990s. Looting became a way of life in poor nations, as it will to us.

A REDISTRIBUTION OF INCOME

Economist A.C. Pigou noted that in all times in all societies, the distribution of income has always been the same within a narrow range. In other words, there have always been the rich and the poor.

But now, like in France in 1789, the rich now have the bulk of their resources invested in Treasury debts since they like low risk and high return investments. The steep fall from favor of public debt will wipe out these holdings and so set the stage for a new ruling elite since societies always have a large division of income and ruling elites. The old wealth and power in America will vanish like it has in other societies in this coming convulsion. And someone else will be in financial command and have the new power.

CHANGE IN OUR BELIEF SYSTEMS

Willis Harmon, in a book entitled *Global Mind Change,* argued that societal transformations are the result of something as simple as a change of mind in the way we perceive events. It is these mind changes that alter the way we look at science, at business, and so on. This, he believed, sets the stage for a dramatic change at the most fundamental level of the belief structures of Western Society. One that, he thought, "was hazardous for civilization...the passengers on planet Earth have a rough passage ahead."[3]

It is a change that promises a spiritual renaissance, some historians have speculated. Lewis Mumford in *The Transformations of Man* believed that there have been about five major transformations of man since the beginning.[4]

He speculated on another transformation of modern society:

"Every (human) transformation...has rested on a new metaphysical and ideological base; or rather, upon deeper stirrings and intuitions whose rationalized expression takes the form of a new picture of the cosmos and the nature of man.... We stand at the brink of such a new age: the age of an open world and of a self capable of playing its part in that large sphere. An age of renewal, when work and leisure and learning and love will unite to produce a fresh form for every stage of life, and a higher trajectory for life as a whole...bringing about a fresh release of spiritual energy."

Arnold Toynbee, in *A Study of History* written in the 1930s and 1940s, made an exhaustive study of the evolution and devolution of civilizations. Most readers of Toynbee think of his as the history's foremost pessimist, but he also wrote of a possible "transfiguration" of modern society into some kind of respiritualized form.

THE NEW, INTEREST-FREE MONEY

The old debts will be gone, mostly unpaid. With that climactic happening, a new currency will emerge as I described in Chapter 12. This alone will change capitalism beyond belief since a lynchpin of capitalism has been compound interest, and now that is gone. The new form of money will guarantee no more drastic ups-and-downs in our economic lives in the future.

Can you profit off those less fortunate in the crisis? No. The penalties for this behavior will be drastic, as they should be.

Critically, our faith in old ideas and the old order will be shaken. Our beliefs, after all, were really just articles of faith of unconscious origin. And now they are transformed. The new era will be different, of course, but it will be, above all, a time of greater challenge and greater hope for everyone to share. We will live through the coming turmoil, as others have in similar times before us. We will also land on our collective feet in the lighted path of the new and challenging age ahead. This will occur because the future did not spring out of a vacuum…the future has already cast its shadow. Now that we know and understand that, we can make personal plans to cope instead of being trapped, as most will, in an unexpected societal breakdown.

CHAPTER FOURTEEN

REFERENCES

1. *Wall Street Journal,* January 2, 1990.

2. *Wall Street Journal,* January 2, 1990.

3 *Global Mind Change.*

4. Lewis Mumford, *The Transformation of Man.*

EPILOGUE

Emerson wrote, "In our society there is a standing antagonism between the conservative and the democratic classes; between those who have made their fortunes, and the young and poor who have fortunes to make; between the interests of dead labor—that is, the labor of hands long ago still in the grave, which labor is now entombed in money stocks, or in land and buildings owned by idle capitalists—and the interests of living labor, which seeks to possess itself of land and buildings and money stocks. The first class is timid, selfish, illiberal, hating innovation, and continually losing numbers by death. The second class is selfish also, encroaching, bold, self-relying, always outnumbering the other and recruiting its numbers every hour by births. It desires to keep open every avenue to the competition of all, and to multiply avenues; the class of business men in America, in England, in France; the class of industry and skill."

We are certain in these emerging hard times to see the eruption of social unrest and violence in America, perhaps on a larger scale than we have seen in a very long time. The reason will be the clash between the conservative and the democratic classes that Emerson wrote about.

You must also prepare yourself financially and psychologically for this coming event. This potential threat makes the idea of living in a rural area have much merit; it enhances the hoarding of gold idea and becoming ever more self-reliant and self-sufficient.

CONSPIRATORS' HIERARCHY:
THE STORY OF THE COMMITTEE OF 300
By Dr. John Coleman... America West Publishers
$16.95... 300pp... Trade Paper... ISBN: 0-922356-57-2

This book, by Dr. John Coleman, former member of MI6, rips the lid off the conspiratorial group which knows NO national boundaries, is ABOVE the laws of ALL countries and controls every aspect of politics, religion, commerce, industry, banking, insurance, mining and even the **drug trade**! Learn how this small Elite group who are answerable to NO ONE, except its members, have pulled the strings on ALL world events and why, until now, few people have even been aware of their existence, let alone power, in manipulating the affairs of the entire WORLD. ALL of these members are revealed, including all of the corporations, government agencies and various movements which "they" have developed and control to further their own aims for WORLD DOMINATION. Find out who is at the seat of power of this octopus of evil whose tentacles reach into your very life and what YOU can do about it!

FREE!

CATALOG

OF RELATED PUBLICATIONS

CALL

(800) 729-4131

OR

WRITE

AMERICA WEST
P. O. BOX 3300
BOZEMAN, MT 59772

QUANTITY DISCOUNTS AVAILABLE

THE TRUTH WILL | SET YOU FREE!